CW01163168

A Bedroom Business

The Life and Times of a Serial Entrepreneur

HARRISON P. FULLER

© 2024 Harrison P. Fuller. All rights reserved.

No part of this book may be reproduced, stored in a retrieval system, or transmitted by any means without the written permission of the author.

AuthorHouse™
1663 Liberty Drive
Bloomington, IN 47403
www.authorhouse.com
Phone: 833-262-8899

Because of the dynamic nature of the Internet, any web addresses or links contained in this book may have changed since publication and may no longer be valid. The views expressed in this work are solely those of the author and do not necessarily reflect the views of the publisher, and the publisher hereby disclaims any responsibility for them.

Any people depicted in stock imagery provided by Getty Images are models, and such images are being used for illustrative purposes only.
Certain stock imagery © Getty Images.

This book is printed on acid-free paper.

ISBN: 979-8-8230-3535-4 (sc)
ISBN: 979-8-8230-3536-1 (hc)
ISBN: 979-8-8230-3534-7 (e)

Library of Congress Control Number: 2024921187

Print information available on the last page.

Published by AuthorHouse 10/29/2024

authorHOUSE

Contents

Introduction 2
Chapter 1   Genesis 7
Chapter 2   The Fuller's 10
Chapter 3   Where it all began 15
Chapter 4   My first Decade 23
Chapter 5   High School 31
Chapter 6   Lehigh University 39
Chapter 7   My Wife, Pat Green 46
Chapter 8   A Traveling Salesman 49
Chapter 9   My Lovable Uncle Marty (Dad's Older Brother) 54
Chapter 10   Marriage and the Military 57
Chapter 11   The Military 60
Chapter 12   Stuttgart, Germany; Kenny and Robert Lonoff 69
Chapter 13   Bill Ferriter 72
Chapter 14   The Rest of (Our) Lives; Becoming an Innovative Entrepreneur 81
Chapter 15   The Bronx 86
Chapter 16   Pine Hollow CC 89
Chapter 17   Discharged 92
Chapter 18   Japan with Jerry Hahn 95
Chapter 19   Steve Gutman 100
Chapter 20   Settlling Down 102
Chapter 21   The 60's 107
Chapter 22   My First Startup (with Training Wheels) 109
Chapter 23   Fun Time 115
Chapter 24   All is Well (until it wasn't) 116

Chapter 25	The Week That Shook My World	122
Chapter 26	June 1967: Unemployed	131
Chapter 27	Filling in the gaps	135
Chapter 28	Brick and Mortar	139
Chapter 29	Lesson Learned	145
Chapter 30	Growing the Business	147
Chapter 31	TRUE VALUE HARDWARE	150
Chapter 32	Family	161
Chapter 33	Health Issues	163
Chapter 34	Back to Business	166
Chapter 35	Business and Pleasure	169
Chapter 36	Too close for comfort	171
Chapter 37	Survival	176
Chapter 38	Heart trouble	179
Chapter 39	A Bedroom Business	181
Chapter 40	Fish or Cut Bait!	186
Chapter 41	The Home Depot	194
Chapter 42	A Musical Recital	202
Chapter 43	A Remarkable Coincidence	203
Chapter 44	Bad Vibes	205
Chapter 45	Their Final Act	208
Chapter 46	Growing Pains	210
Chapter 47	Moving On	213
Chapter 48	Madoff and Me	215
Chapter 49	"Find a Need and Package It!	218
Chapter 50	THE TRUTH WILL OUT!	220
Epilogue		224

A Bedroom Business

The Life and Times of a Serial Entrepreneur

The Home Depot, Lowe's Home Centers, and TrueValue Hardware never knew their mulitimillion dollar supplier was run by a married couple from their spare bedroom.

Introduction

My sister sent me a record of our family history from nineteenth-century Russia, Poland, and Hungary to Ellis Island in the United States.

What it did not, and could not, reveal was what our long-gone relatives had accomplished after they arrived in America.

I realized that my grandson Maxwell, his future children, and great grandchildren, deserve to know more than the dates of birth and death of family members once we, too, are gone.

Although initially written for my own family and friends, I hope it will inspire others to write their own personal histories. Your future generations will thank you.

Note: I refer to my father in various ways including as Bennie, Bernard, BF, BHF, Dad, and the Boss. I am either Harrison, or Buzz, or Buzzy. My older sister is sometimes Dorothy, Dee, Dotty, or Deborah.

Children of My Generation (anonymous)

Born in the 1930s, we are the "Silent Generation."

We are the last generation who spent their entire childhood without television.

Social media had not been invented yet.

On Saturday afternoons, newsreels of World War 2 were shown between movie serials, Westerns, and Disney cartoons.

Telephones were one to a house and often shared via party lines.

Every store had a cash register. There were no credit cards.

Typewriters were driven by pounding fingers, throwing the carriage, and changing the ribbon.

We got the daily news from the newspaper.

Our parents were suddenly free from the confines of the Depression and the war, and they threw themselves into exploring opportunities they had never imagined.

Polio was still a crippler, but Dr. Salk discovered a vaccine.

The Korean War was a dark presage in the early 1950s and by mid-decade, schoolchildren were ducking under desks for air raid training.

Eisenhower sent the first "advisers" to Vietnam.

We grew up at a time when the world seemed to be getting better, not worse.

We are the Silent Generation.

More than 90 percent of us are retired or deceased. We feel privileged to have "lived in the good times."

Coming to America

I always wondered how and why my grandparents left Europe and made the difficult journey to America. Can you imagine leaving your family and the familiar surroundings you have known your entire life?

Think of it.

Unfortunately, like other immigrants, my relatives rarely spoke about this part of their lives. They never talked about the hardships they endured traveling to America. The spoke only Yiddish. There was no money, few jobs, and poor housing. Disease, poverty, and prejudice surrounded them for the first few years.

Jewish immigrants provided their children with an education. Their children became scientists, businesspeople, political leaders, teachers, actors, and doctors. In America, anything was possible.

My grandparents were born in Europe in the late 1800s. They had endured poverty and rampant anti-Semitism. In the small villages where most were from, there was no electricity, no indoor plumbing, no cars, and no telephones. It was a world long gone and not missed.

Coming to America was a difficult decision, not just for themselves, but for their parents, too. Years later, 99 percent of those who remained behind, or couldn't get out, perished in the Holocaust.

My father's stories about his childhood and his family were rare and mostly meant to amuse. My mother never shared much about her own childhood and little about other family members. However, on both sides, there were many aunts, uncles, and cousins that we visited fairly frequently.

My grandparents revealed nothing about their former lives and the conditions that drove them to emigrate. There was only silence. My questions were answered with stories about this or that relative. What I wanted to know was how and why my grandparents came to America? What was life like in the old country? What was life like for poor immigrants in the late 1800s? Did they come with their parents or alone? We will never have answers to such questions.

Today, we use DNA to trace our genealogy, but real life is not revealed in strands of DNA. One's life cannot be viewed through a microscope. It must be on a written document.

My own history began when Franklin Roosevelt was in his first year as president. The Great Depression was still raging. There were no televisions, personal computers, or iPhones.

This is the story of my own life and times. I have tried to give a little perspective by including important national and international events that occurred along the way.

This book is dedicated to my wife Pat, my children, David and Susan, their spouses Rachel and Julie, and to my grandson Max, plus anyone who may be interested.

It is the story of a second-generation American, born in the 1930s, and the grandchild of immigrants.

As these are my personal recollections, they do not always align with how others may recall the same events.

Chapter 1
Genesis

In the 1890s, the Russian tsar expelled Jews from most Russian cities. Pogroms resulted in the slaughter of hundreds of thousands. Émile Zola published an expose of anti-Semitism in France about the Dreyfus Affair.

My maternal grandfather, Jacob Manchyk, was born in Poland around 1880, during the time of pogroms and poverty in the shtetels in Poland and Russia. There was no difference which side of the Polish-Russian border you lived on. Either way, life was hard and short.

For a young man, the possibility of being forced into the Russian army was real. Like many others of his generation, Grandpa Jake became a tailor. This was a useful profession that would enable him to make a decent living, in Europe or America.

At the age of eighteen or so, Jake left home and made his way from eastern Poland to Ellis Island. We don't have any details about the voyage, but it surely was long and difficult.

We do know, however, that upon arriving in New York City, his dream of going west and meeting real cowboys overtook him. For the next eighteen months, Jake traveled about the west, supporting himself with small tailoring jobs. He met some real cowboys, but quickly realized that he was not meant to be a cowboy. He barely spoke or understood the language. He was an Orthodox Jew and strictly kosher. Jacob Manchyk returned to Manhattan, where he married Anna Liebowitz.

Grandpa Jake passed away a few days before my bar mitzvah in January 1947. He might have been sixty-seven years old, but to me, he seemed much older.

I know very little about the origins of my maternal grandmother Anna (née Leibowitz) Manchyk. I was told she was born in Minsk and came here around 1895 with her family.

Wilbur Wright made the first solo airplane flight, and construction began on the Panama Canal. In 1907 in England, suffragettes stormed Parliament. 11,745 immigrants came through Ellis Island, and the financial panic of 1907 started a depression.

Anna Leibowitz married Jacob Manchyk in1902. Their first child, Bertha, was born in 1904. My own mother, Helen was born in 1907. The last child, Gilbert Manchyk, arrived in 1912.

Gilbert was college educated, intellectual, and like both of his parents, had a calm disposition. Gilbert married my Aunt Norma, about whom I know nothing except that she was tall and striking with long black hair. Norma died quite young. She had two daughters whom I never met.

The growing Manchyk family lived in the Washington Heights section of Manhattan, long before the George Washington Bridge was built. Grandma Anna kept a kosher home. Her two daughters, Helen and Bertha, followed the tradition.

Jacob Manchyk, my maternal grandfather, born in Poland 1873, died 1946 in New York City. Wife Anna Leibowitz from Ukraine born 1884, died 1969

Chapter 2
The Fuller's

The Fuller side had a far different history. I never met my paternal grandfather Harris Fuller (or Filler). My grandmother Hermina was only around for two or three years of my life, but I did hear a few stories about her from my father.

After all the children were in bed, she would cook her wonderful strudel. My father also revealed that my mother Helen and his mother Hermina did not get along well at all. No surprise there.

Both paternal grandparents were born in nineteenth-century Austria, far from Vienna in the countryside.

Anti-Semitism was extreme, possibly the worst in all of Europe and Russia. The "Filler" family left Europe along with millions of others.

Unlike Russian and Polish Jews, Austro-Hungarian Jews were from coal and iron mining areas. They were involved in metalworking, producing kitchen and hardware items.

My father's father was named Herchel (Harris). Either he or another relative changed the name from Filler to Fuller. In New York, "Hersch" found work as a presser in the garment industry. It would take his son Bennie to revive the hardware tradition of the old country.

My father, Bernard (Bennie) Fuller was born on the Lower East Side of Manhattan on July 19, 1907.

The family relocated to a different tenement every few months because they frequently could not pay the rent.

Bernard was the second youngest of eleven children. The oldest sister, Annie, was a half-sister. Their father had been married once before and had a daughter named Anna by his first wife. I assume he was a widower, however, no record exists that could prove why Anna was with her father, not her mother.

Aunt Annie was twenty-five years old and married when my father was born. My father was only six months older than Annie's son, Milton Davis. The two boys became close friends.

Children of Harris Tzvi Hersch Filler and Hermina Rosenbaum

#	Name	Born	Died	Age
1.	Annie	b. 1882	d. 1953	age 68
2.	Abraham	b. 1883	d. 1961	age 83
3.	Joseph	b. 1894	d. 1971	age 77
4.	Pauline	b. 1897	d. 1981	age 84
5.	Sallie	b. 1899	d. 1985	age 86
6.	Marty	b. 1900	d. 1984	age 84
7.	Fred	b. 1902	d. 1975	age 73
8.	Gertrude	b. 1904	d. 1999	age 95
9.	Helen	b. 1906	d. 2001	age 95
10.	Bernard	b. 1907	d. 2003	age 96
11.	Lilian	b. 1909	d. 1989	age 80

My father, Bennie, as he was then called, was just seven years old when his father died. My grandfather's demise was due to tuberculosis, then a very common cause of death. His tenth child, my own father, passed away at ninety-six, having lived longer than anyone else in his immediate family.

The story goes that their widowed mother, Hermina, had so little confidence in her youngest son that when their father died, she urged an older son, Fred, to look after Bennie.

The metalworking tradition of Hungary would soon come to America. In 1935, Bernie Fuller and his brother Fred established Fuller Brothers, manufacturers of hand tools and cutlery.

Over the years, Bernie became more successful than any of his siblings, and in fact helped many of them with jobs and financial support. It is ironic that his mother had so little confidence in her youngest son.

My parents were both were in their teens when they met.

Bernie was a poor kid from the Lower East Side. They lived on Pitkin Avenue, Delancy Street, and several other locations. Helen lived in relative splendor uptown in Washington Heights. The year was 1925 and they were both eighteen years old.

In 1925, Mussolini became dictator of Italy. President Calvin Coolidge was inaugurated. The Scopes Monkey Trial ended in a conviction for teaching evolution.

Unfortunately, Helen did not inherit her parents' calm disposition. She was overly critical, demanding, and impossible to please. At the time, I thought all mothers were like my own. In retrospect, it seems clear to me that she most likely suffered from clinical depression. This made her unsuitable for motherhood.

My father seemed to be "in charge," but it was really Helen who made every family decision. In those days, a Jewish wife could not be perceived as the "head of the family." That was the father's job. Consequently, although Bernie was the "enforcer," the family knew that Mother decided how things would be at home. In his office, Bernie was the boss.

In those days, using the New York City subway, you could travel from the Lower East Side to Washington Heights for a nickel. When he had a date with Helen, Bernie spent the time and money to make the trip to Washington Heights.

After graduating from high school, Helen attended City College and worked as a teller in a bank.

The story was that Helen had "set her cap" for Bernie and was determined to marry him. They were married on June 21, 1931. Both were twenty-four years old.

In 1931, the Empire State Building opened. Japan invaded Chinese Manchuria, and the George Washington Bridge opened. Franklin Roosevelt was first inaugurated. First-class postage cost three cents, and the Lindbergh baby was kidnapped.

My older sister Dorothy was born in Manhattan on May 7, 1932.

That same year, Adolf Hitler consolidated his power over the German state and began to systematically purge Jews from the professions, hospitals, universities, arts, science, and business.

Commercial flight was in its infancy. There were not yet any scheduled airlines or consumer flights.

New York streets still smelled of the manure of horses drawing carts. Coal was the primary fuel for heating homes and businesses. Refrigerators required a large block of fresh ice every few days. If you had an icebox, you were fortunate. The telephone was a standing device with a rotary dial in the base.

Radio stations featured daily serials. For kids, there was *The Lone Ranger*, *Mr. District Attorney*, and *Inner Sanctum* with the squeaky door. President Franklin Roosevelt was in his first term. Fiorello LaGuardia was the popular mayor of New York City.

It was the Great Depression and millions of Americans were unemployed. Men waited in long breadlines or simply begged for food. Social Security did not yet exist.

Germany secretly began to rebuild its military. Hitler instituted the Nuremberg Laws, which stripped Jews of their civil rights. Mussolini ordered his newly acquitted German Junkers and bombed civilians in Ethiopia.

In Spain, Francisco Franco became the newest member of the Axis, along with Hitler and Mussolini.

A reformed drinker named Bill Wilson started Alcoholics Anonymous. Dupont created Nylon, the first synthetic fiber. Persia became Iran.

Chapter 3
Where it all began

I was born on January 9, 1934, at Brooklyn Jewish Hospital during the coldest winter New York has ever experienced, before or since. In that same year, Babe Ruth signed a $3,400 annual contract with the Boston Red Sox. The prison at Alcatraz opened. Bonnie Parker and Clyde Barrow started robbing banks.

My mother Helen was twenty-seven and my father was a few months older. Despite hard times, Bernie had a good job as a salesman for the new Staybrite Company. He sold stainless steel cutlery to "jobbers" for resale to hardware and housewares stores. It was a great new product. Until then, cutlery was made of carbon steel and would quickly rust. Stainless steel was unaffected by water and remained bright, hence the name, the Staybrite Cutlery Company.

The new American president, Franklin Delano Roosevelt, had promised the country a new deal, and it seemed possible. He took office in 1933 and died in 1945 during his fourth term.

At my birth, we lived in a small, two-family house in Brooklyn. It was near a schoolyard, which was fenced off at the end of our street.

The Brooklyn Jewish Center was close by on Kings Highway. One night, there was a large fire a few blocks away. My father took me to the schoolyard fence and from there, we watched a house burn down. That seems to be my earliest memory with my father.

There are few interesting things that I recall during my brief time in Brooklyn. These included the Brooklyn Dodgers, Leo Durocher, and Joe Lewis ("Jolting Joe"). I listened to the radio after school. To most kids of my generation, baseball was a big deal. We were vaguely aware of Adolf Hitler and anti-Jewish laws in Germany, but that was far away and of not a concern for a boy of five living in Flatbush, a mostly Jewish section of Brooklyn in New York City.

Sometime in 1939 or 1940, we moved from Brooklyn to a single-family house with a separate garage and a garden. It was at 223rd Street and 138th Avenue in Laurelton, Queens.

My grammar school was PS 156. I later learned this was the same grammar school attended by Bernie and Ruth Madoff, although they were a few years younger than me. The school was about ten blocks from home and I enjoyed the walk.

After school, there was an hour of Hebrew school at the Laurelton Jewish Center. Television was not even a dream. We had our own telephone although many others used a party line. This meant you shared a telephone line with another household. If the other party was using the phone, you waited until it was free.

The house in Laurelton was small although it had four bedrooms. There was a small backyard and a one-car garage. My dad paid $7,000. Today, our house in Laurelton would likely fetch $400,000.

Some of my Laurelton friends were Rennie Korn (now a lawyer), Arnie Gliet, Everet Kavaler (our dentist's son), David Robbins (Dr. Robbins's son), Louie Gilmore (a good athlete), Stanley Matlick (his father owned Zelinka Matlick Company, which sold high-end women's clothes), and Harriet Goldberg (her mother seemed old—maybe forty).

We had a Buick with a stick shift. It was a beauty. Many Sundays were spent washing the car with a bucket of soap and water and a few rags. During the war years, you needed a special exemption (a B sticker) to buy a few gallons of gas.

Every other Sunday, we would take the family Buick up to Washington Heights to Grandma Manchyk's apartment on Arden Street. The car was always sparkly clean.

Aunt Bertha, her husband David Wiener, and my cousins Phylis and Joel, would be there. On Passover, Grandpa Jacob, in full Orthodox mode, would lead the family in a four-hour rendition of the Passover Seder. I was only concerned with trying to figure out where the matzah was hidden.

On the forty-minute drive back to Laurelton, I would fall asleep in the back of the Buick.

On other occasions, we would visit my Uncle Marty (one of Dad's brothers), Marty's wife Kitty, daughter Judy, and son Harris. They also lived in Washington Heights.

One Sunday afternoon in December 1941, my uncle Gilbert (Mother's younger brother) and his wife Norma, came for Sunday dinner at our house. Our big Stromberg Carlson radio was tuned to 1560, WQXR, the only classical music station for New York City. The women were preparing dinner, and my dad and Uncle Gilbert were listening to the radio. I was standing silently next to them.

Suddenly, the radio announcer interrupted the music. He said there had been a sneak attack on the US fleet in Pearl Harbor. Everyone stopped what they were doing and focused on the radio. The atmosphere had become somber. Where was Pearl Harbor, and why did the Japanese bomb American ships? All I knew about Japan was the cheap metal toys I loved to play with.

World War 2 was declared in early December 1941. One month later in January 1942, I turned eight years old.

During World War 1, twenty-three years earlier in 1918, my father was eleven years old.

In 1941, he was thirty-four and married with two children. He would not be required to join the war.

World War 2 brought big changes to our neighborhood. None of the other men on our street were drafted as they were either too old or married with kids. My father's new company, Fuller Tool, made screwdrivers, a product considered necessary to the war effort.

At least once a week, there were air raid drills. During a drill, we turned off the house lights and lowered the black shades. The idea was to keep from being a target of Nazi bombers. Every street had an air raid warden who wore a steel hat and patrolled the street to be sure every house was dark.

For me, the war years were memorable. We collected tin cans and anything made of rubber, planted a victory garden for fresh vegetables, and went to war bond rallies.

Years later while in college, I learned that the reason for war bonds was to prevent inflation caused by excess cash for which there were few consumer products. War bonds soaked up the excess cash.

In addition, war bonds provided the government with the money to finance the weapons required to defeat the Axis powers of Japan, Germany, Italy, and some of the German-occupied countries.

As the family business, Fuller Tool Company, was a large part of my life, and had a huge influence on my later life and career, a bit of background is necessary.

Fuller Brothers Tools and Cutlery was formed in 1938 as a partnership between Fred Fuller (a brother) and my father, Bernard Fuller.

Between 1937 and 1938, industrial production in the United States fell 30 percent and unemployment rose to 19 percent.

On October 10, 1938 (Kristallnacht), Jewish stores and houses of worship were vandalized and destroyed throughout Germany.

Fred had been a salesman for a new type of glass cutter. Bernie had started out during the Great Depression as a salesman for Staybrite (stainless steel) Cutlery. Pooling their talents and a few hundred dollars, they started Fuller Brothers Tools and Cutlery.

The new company assembled stainless steel knife blades, imported from Sheffield, England, into a line of low-cost carving sets and steak knives. Bernie would call on the houseware "jobbers" he knew as a salesman with Staybrite Cutlery Company.

From his days selling glass cutters, Uncle Fred knew all the hardware distributors in New York and New Jersey.

In addition to cutlery, the original line of Fuller tools consisted of six sizes of slotted and Phillips head screwdrivers, all with dark wood handles.

The brothers operated the business in a in a loft on West 23rd near Broadway in Manhattan.

Within a year, Bernie said that the company could not support two families. Fred was happy to sell his 50 percent share to Bernie for $500.

Fred moved to Miami Beach, where he owned a successful hardware store for fifty years. He became the unofficial "Mayor of Alton Avenue."

Sadly, after Fred left, the two brothers never spoke to each other again. Helen Fuller always said, "Once you leave, you can't ever come back."

Note: In April 2007, I emailed Uncle Fred's son, Harris. I wanted to know his recollection of the breakup of Fuller Brothers. How did it come to pass that his father Fred and Bernie split up less than one year after starting Fuller Brothers?

This is the email reply I received from Fred's son, my cousin Harris Fuller.

>   To: hfuller@optonline.net
>   Subject: RE: cousins
>   Harrison Fuller
>   Sent: Thursday, April 26, 2007 2:39 p.m.
>   Subject: Fuller Bros.
>
>
>   Dear Buzz
>
>   I will do my best to respond to your inquiry.
>
>   The way I understand it, Fred was asked by their mother never to abandon Bernie in any business dealings because she thought Bernie wasn't too

swift. When he got very sick, Bernie was very insistent that it was in (Fred's) best interest to sell his share of Fuller Brothers Ltd. to Bernie.

Bernie scared the hell out of Fred with the thought that Fred's family would be left out in the cold with nothing. With Fred in poor health, he was frightened that Bernie would screw them out of their legacy. Fred sold out to Bernie and lived happily ever after in Miami Beach. They never spoke to each other again.

Personally, I think some is bullshit and some is real. I do not know the real truth and never will.

In addition, I don't care. My father was not the greatest guy in the world. He left me with more than my share of scars, non physical.

Fortunately, I was married to a wonderful woman for over forty-eight years and overcame the crap of the past. I do not miss my father or mother, but I do miss my Connie.

I probably went somewhat off course for my not so good explanation. For that I apologize.

Whatever the two of them did to each other, we, the children, lost out. I never really knew my cousins except the AH of western civilization, Peter the Schmuck, and that's a shame.

If I can think of anything else. I will pass it on.

Your Cousin, Harris Fuller

The *schmuck* was Peter Metzger, the son of my father's sister Gertrude (née Fuller) Metzger. Peter was a scientist who specialized in the safe storage of nuclear waste.

Uncle Fred was the first family member to join the business and the first shown the door.

Chapter 4
My first Decade

The days were filled with grade school, Hebrew school, and piano lessons. My friends and I would take the Q5 bus to Jamaica Avenue. Gertz Department Store and the Valencia Theater, built in the 1920s. were on Jamaica Avenue along with the elevated subway. The Valencia featured a black, nighttime "sky" with "stars" twinkling and moving clouds. The Valencia had only first-run movies. You could spend the day watching two movies for twenty-five cents. The Valencia was the first move theater that had "refrigerated air." On a hot summer day, my friends and I would linger outside the lobby and enjoy the cool air emanating from inside the theater. My favorite stars were Humphrey Bogart, James Cagney, and Mickey Rooney.

June 6, 1944 was D-Day.

The US army, under General Dwight Eisenhower, landed on the beaches of Normandy, France. It was the beginning of the end of World War 2.

I was ten years old. Under the watchful eye of Kal Spears (Fuller Tool factory manager), I swept the factory floor, assembled handles onto pocket-sized screwdrivers, and learned how to pour hot glue into "stag" handles of carving knives and forks.

The big American tool brands, such as Stanley and Cooper, were busy producing essential products for the war effort.

Bernie Fuller had no desire to supply the US government and used the lack of competitors to supply screwdrivers (its only hardware product) to desperate hardware distributors cut off from their prewar suppliers. The war had diverted American tool companies, including Stanley, Cooper, Disston, and others from the domestic market. Fuller Tool screwdrivers were suddenly in demand.

Most evenings after dinner, we would listen on the radio for the progress of the war. We learned about the Marines landing on Wake Island and General Rommel's defeat by British General Montgomery and US General George Patton in North Africa.

I built a crystal radio and tried to pick up Nazi submarines stationed near Long Island. Finally, after four years, Germany surrendered in May 1945. A few months later, after Truman dropped two atomic bombs on Hiroshima and Nagasaki, the Japanese surrendered. 1945 was the end of my childhood.

By the time World War 2 was over, Fuller Tool Company had secured a foothold in the hardware industry and would never look back. Detroit resumed production of new automobiles the most popular cars were Ford, Chevrolet, and Hudson. The most expensive were Packard and Cadillac. A new car was introduced and quickly became sucessful. It was the Studebaker. You didn't know if it was coming or going.

The Triborough Bridge and the Queens Midtown Tunnel tolls were twenty-five cents. The Verrazano and Throggs Neck Bridges were still many years away.

In 1944, an experienced business executive was considered well paid if he earned $10,000 per year. Our three-bedroom house in the suburb of Laurelton, Queens, on a fifty-foot by one-hundred-foot lot cost $7,000.

My first car, a 1951 (brown) Dodge with stick shift, cost $1,200 new.

No self-respecting middle-class Jewish mother of the era would deny her children music lessons.

Both my older sister and I took piano lessons. We were forced to practice for thirty minutes every day. We did our scales and played Chopin's études. Our teacher was Mr. Schoenwetter, who drove a Hudson.

Mr. S. tried hard to teach us. Although talent ran in the family (Aunt Bertha, my cousin Phylis's mother, always played "Happy Birthday"), piano lessons never bore fruit. I also studied the violin for a few years, but that effort proved as fruitless as piano lessons.

Although my mother wanted me to audition for Juilliard, I knew it would be a disaster. I remain, to this day, an ardent lover of classical music. For my entire life, music has never been far from wherever I happen to be. I am considered a gifted "air conductor."

> We saw the 'boys' home from the war build their Cape Cod style houses, pouring t>he cellar, tar papering it over and living there until they could afford the time and >money to build it out.
>
>
> We are the last who spent childhood without television; instead imagining what >we heard on the radio. As we all like to brag, with no TV, we spent our childhood >"playing outside until the street lights came on." We did play outside and we did >play on our own. There was no little league.
>
>
> The lack of television in our early years meant, for most of us, that we had little >real understanding of what the world was like. Our Saturday afternoons, if at the >movies, gave us newsreels of the war and the holocaust sandwiched in between >westerns and cartoons. Newspapers and magazines were written for adults. We >are the last who had to find out for ourselves.
>
> As we grew up, the country was exploding with growth. The G.I. Bill gave >returning veterans the means to get an education and spurred colleges to grow. >VA loans fanned a housing boom. Pent up demand coupled with new installment >payment plans put factories to work. New highways would bring jobs and >mobility. The veterans joined civic clubs and became active in politics. In the late >40s and early 50's the country seemed to lie in the embrace of brisk but quiet >order as it gave birth to its new middle class. Our parents understandably >became absorbed with their own new lives. They were free from the confines of >the depression and the war. They threw themselves into exploring opportunities >they had never imagined.
>
> We weren't neglected but we weren't today's all-consuming family focus. They >were glad we played by ourselves 'until the street lights came on.' They were >busy discovering the post war world.
>
> Most of us had no life plan, but with the unexpected virtue of ignorance and an >economic rising tide we simply stepped into the world and went to find out. We >entered a world of overflowing plenty and opportunity; a world where we were >welcomed. Based on our naïve belief that there was more where this came from, >we shaped life as we went.
>
> We enjoyed a luxury; we felt secure in our future. Of course, just as today, not all >Americans shared in this experience. Depression poverty was deep rooted. >Polio was still a crippler. The Korean War was a dark presage in the early 50s and >by mid-decade school children were ducking under desks. China became Red >China. Eisenhower sent the first 'advisors' to Vietnam. Castro set up camp in >Cuba and Khrushchev came to power.
>
> We are the last to experience an interlude when there were no existential threats >to our homeland. We came of age in the late 40s and early 50s. The war was over >and the cold war, terrorism, climate change, technological upheaval and >perpetual economic insecurity had yet to haunt life with insistent unease.
>
> Only we can remember both a time of apocalyptic war and a time when our world >was secure and full of bright promise and plenty. We experienced both.
>
> We grew up at the best possible time, a time when the world was getting better >not worse.

The above essay is unattributed, but accurate.

In the summer of 1945, I was an eleven-year-old at Camp Cejwin. We observed the Sabbath by wearing white "ducks," singing songs, and eating kosher food.

On August 12, 1945, the camp director announced that an atomic bomb had been dropped on Hiroshima, Japan. We had no idea why another bomb dropped on a Japanese city was worth a special announcement. To me and my mates, it was just a bigger bomb.

After the war, we learned that six million Jews had been systematically rounded up and murdered by the Nazis between 1939 and 1945. The Nuremberg Trials in 1946 were the first attempt to recognize genocide as a war crime, and to punish those responsible.

Second Decade

One of my starkest memories of being eleven was a vicious fight with three Gentile boys from the next town, Springfield Gardens. I was approached on the way home from school. They began taunting me with "You killed Christ" repeatedly. Of course, I had no idea what they were talking about. They threw stones and one of them started swinging at me with a leather belt. We pushed and wrestled with each other. I was a good fighter, bigger and older than either of them. All the while, they kept calling me "Kike," a dirty Jew, and Christ killer.

I suddenly experienced violent anti-Semitism. At the time, we lived in a quiet, peaceful, and mostly Jewish community. Some would call it a gilded ghetto, although it was hardly "gilded." The encounter and the slurs were a revelation, and the experience has stayed with me.

One fine Autumn day, to my surprise and everyone else's, my mother announced she was pregnant and due the following June. On June 21, 1945, June Fuller was born at a small hospital in Kew Gardens. Long Island Jewish Hospital and North Shore Hospital in Great Neck were not built yet. That would take several more years. In 1945, hospitals outside of Manhattan were usually small, private institutions.

"Today I am a man" was the opening line of my bar mitzvah speech. By today's standards, my bar mitzvah on January 25, 1947 at the Laurelton Jewish Center was a modest affair. The night before the service, I awoke with the knowledge that Grandpa Jacob (Jake) had died. It turned out to be true, which was a bit weird. I really felt bad that he did not survive long enough to see his oldest grandson bar mitzvah.

I recited my Torah portion without a hitch, as did the other boy. Rabbi Teplitz had just graduated from the Jewish Theological Seminary, and we were his first congregation. I was his very first bar mitzvah. At the luncheon that followed, complete with an ice-sculptured swan, surrounded by chopped liver, I delivered my speech. Lunch was served (challah, soup, and chicken) to seventy-five relatives, friends, and worshipers. After lunch, we went back to the small house on 223rd Street. January 25, 1947, was a record warm day, almost sixty-five degrees.

At my bar mitzvah, I received quite a few US government savings bonds as well as cash.

My mother deposited the cash into my first savings account. (Years later, I used my bar mitzvah money to buy a 1950 two-door Dodge with a stick shift. It cost $1,500.)

Now that I was bar mitzvah, I was expected to continue my religious education and to *daven* every day. It didn't happen.

In 1945, with the arrival of my baby sister June, my folks decided we needed a larger house. I still had a few months before the end of seventh grade at PS 156 in Laurelton. It was too late to transfer to PS 131 in Jamaica Estates, so my dad hired a driver to get me to class in Laurelton by 9:00 a.m. every weekday. I could take the Q5 bus back to Hillside Ave and Midland Parkway home. The new house was at the top of small hill on a full acre. It was a ranch house and a lot nicer than our former house. There was even an apple orchard in the back yard.

My bedroom was directly under the roof and during the hot summer months, sleep became impossible. Air conditioning was not yet available. My sister Dorothy's bedroom was larger, cooler, and faced the orchard and the garden. We shared the small bathroom.

Jamaica Estates was a big step up from Laurelton. The Estates was then populated by upper-income families. Most of the homes were on half-acre or larger plots and had four to six bedrooms. The biggest of all was a white colonial with two large columns in front. The house belonged to Fred Trump, Donald Trump's father. I never met Donald as he was fourteen years younger.

Hillcrest Jewish Center was close by on Union Turnpike. It was led by Rabbi Moshowitz, who officiated at the wedding of my sister Dorothy to Jerry Hahn on December 17, 1951. They were married at the Pierre Hotel. The 450-person affair was catered by Katimsky and Tuchman, at the time the best kosher caterers in New York City.

Christmas Vacation, December 1947

The trip to Florida took three days in the family Buick with my parents and sisters. We traveled with Murray and Helen Rubien and their son Johnny. The Rubiens were close friends of my parents from Brooklyn before the war. Murray Rubien was a successful attorney. His wife Helen was an artist and intellectual. They were both very interesting to be around.

Johnny Rubien was two years older them me, a good swimmer, and all-around athlete. He was also an A student. Everyone believed he had a bright future. During our stay in Miami, I mostly hung around Johnny. (As an adult, Johnny Rubien failed at everything he tried. He died at the age of fifty. The highlight of Johnny's life was graduating with honors in the class of 1953 of Columbia University.)

Driving to Florida, along narrow state and county roads, we saw "colored people" dragging long canvas bags of hand-picked cotton. In Georgia, black prisoners were chained together, working on the roadside under the constant glare of white police officers with long rifles riding high on horses. Jim Crow was alive and well.

We stayed at the old Truman Hotel in what is now South Beach. The trip back to New York took only two days, in total silence.

In 1948, the state of Israel was established; war followed. President Harry Truman was reelected for second term. The Berlin Wall was erected. Riding on the New York City subway was still only a nickel. Congress authorized the Marshall Plan for Europe.

Chapter 5
High School

In those days, Jamaica High was a highly respected institution in the New York educational system and known for its successful sports teams. The swim team attracted my attention, in no small part because its members got to wear bright silk swim team jackets. Qualifying for the team was another matter.

These were exciting days if you were Jewish. The state of Israel had barely been proclaimed and recognized by the United States and Russia when a war broke out between all the Arab states and little Israel. My father was already a member of the Zionist Organization of America (ZOA), a political action committee dedicated to the establishment of a Jewish homeland in Palestine. During the First Arab-Israeli War, he procured weapons for the defense of Israel, attended secret meetings, and worked to bring Jews (displaced persons) from the camps in Europe to Israel.

Later, the Bernard and Helen Fuller Foundation became a generous supporter of UJA, Technion, Hadassah Hospital, and other Isreali institutions. The foundation purchased Israel bonds and donated significant sums to UJA.

Burt Rockaway

Burt was from Flushing, Queens, where his father owned a candy store. The store was open seven days a week from 6:00 a.m. to 10:00 p.m. That left little time for anything else,

Burt was always anxious to get away from the store and there was good bus service between Flushing and Union Turnpike. We would hang out at Charney's Deli, the local movie theater, and the Chinese restaurant, where we could have soup, egg roll, and shrimp for $1.95 plus all the white rice we could eat. We went to Young Judea meetings, attended temple dances to meet girls, and did whatever young guys did to keep from being bored. Now those days are in my rear-view mirror.

Through the influence of my Dorothy (she preferred to be known as Deborah), Burt and I became members of Young Judea.

Young Judea was an organization that supported *aliyah*, or the settlement of Israel by American Jews in the diaspora. At the age of fourteen, I spent the summer on a kibbutz camp in New York state. We worked a small farm and built two outhouses and a shower. We lived in tents and learned how to set up a defense perimeter in case of an Arab attack. We were subjected to indoctrinating lectures about the communal life and the happiness we would have when we emigrated to Israel. The co-ed kibbutz was a learning experience for a fifteen-year-old boy.

After four weeks during the summer of 1949 on a kibbutz, I decided that life on a farm in Israel was not for me. However, when a leadership position opened at Young Judea, I ran for president of the Long Island chapter and won.

Long Island Young Judea had a membership of several hundred teenagers. The president was required to implement the program determined by the national organization. They set the agenda, but the local president had to implement it. There were speakers from Israel, committees set up to raise funds for Israel, and efforts to recruit new members. The experience taught me how to lead, how to implement new ideas, and how to improve my public speaking.

A Bit about Music

As a teenager, I was interested classical music, girls, and golf, in no order.

Having studied the violin, I auditioned for the Jamaica High school orchestra. It was fun but the orchestra was awful. However, it gave me an appreciation of what a real pianist or violinist must do to achieve artistry. While I could not perform myself, I listened to WQXR, 1560 on the AM dial, to hear the greatest composers and performers. Music has been an important part of my life ever since.

Golf. My mother introduced me to the game of golf, which I have enjoyed all my life. How, when, and why did Helen Fuller as a young mother learn to play golf? During the war years when gas was rationed, she took the bus, carrying her golf clubs, to the nearby public golf course and played until the sun went down.

What interest would the daughter of poor immigrants have in the upscale (expensive) white-collar game of golf? Who taught her? I don't know, but it surely wasn't my father, who never mastered any aspect of the game, although not for lack of trying.

In 1949, soon after moving to Jamaica Estates, my folks joined Cold Spring Harbor Country Club. I was fifteen years old and anxious to learn the game. After just one year, we left Cold Spring Country Club and joined the newly opened Pine Hollow Country Club in East Norwich, New York.

I took golf lessons from the club pro, Pat Tiso, and played eighteen holes every weekend. I even won a few tournaments.

In 1949 over the Christmas holidays, I went on a Caribbean cruise with my parents. Dorothy was more interested in boys, especially Jerry Hahn, and stayed home with her little sister, June.

My tiny cabin was almost at the bottom of the ship, close to the engine room, which made sleeping difficult. When we arrived in the tropics, the lack of air conditioning added to my discomfort.

The ship stopped at Freeport in the Bahamas and at least six islands before eventually arriving in Havana, Cuba.

There are two things worth mentioning at this point.

1. In 1949, Havana was still controlled by Batista, a corrupt leader who was universally despised by the Cuban people but loved by the upper classes. One year later, in 1950, he would be overthrown by Fidel Castro.

2. Once the ship docked, my father asked Johnny Weil, a thirty-two year-old bachelor he had just met, to show me the sights of Havana. Johnny was fun to be around and very anxious to visit the tourist joints and brothels that Havana was then noted for. Johnny took me under his wing; it was a learning experience.

On our return to New York, my father hired Johnny Weil as the sales manager of Fuller Tool Company. It was a good decision—probably his best.

Jerry Hann married my sister Dorothy, she was just nineteen and he was twenty. My parents were not happy about her choice.

Jerry Hahn was raised in Brooklyn and lived with his folks (Irving and Viola) in a small house north of Union Turnpike. When he started dating my sister Dorothy, Jerry had just graduated from Pace University, where he studied advertising. My folks thought it was an inappropriate marriage as there was little chance that he would be able to support my sister "in the manner to which she had become accustomed." However, Dad would give Jerry a chance to prove himself.

Upon their return from Bermuda, Bernie split his small company into two divisions: Fuller Tool Company and Fuller Cutlery Company. Jerry was put to work at the new cutlery company, although his father-in-law would retain control.

Jerry turned out to be a very good businessman. He had an obvious talent for advertising, marketing, and sales. Within a few years, Bernie let him run the cutlery division on his own.

Under Jerry's leadership, Regent Sheffield grew into one of the most successful companies in its field. Long before the marriage dissolved, Jerry had negotiated the separation of Regent Sheffield from Fuller Tool Company. At the time of their divorce, Jerry was the sole owner of Regent Sheffield Ltd., much to the chagrin of my parents.

Jerry passed away at the age of seventy-one. However, before he died, he sold Regent Sheffield to an Australian company for quite a large sum. For the next five or so years, Jerry Hahn followed in the footsteps of his two older sons and became an orthodox Jew.

As with any endeavor he undertook, Jerry immersed himself in the subject. He became a scholar of Jewish history and even wrote a book on the subject. He was joined in his pursuit of Jewish orthodoxy by his beautiful new wife, Lynn. From the day we met her, Lynn Hahn became part of our family.

Jerry Hahn achieved more in life than anyone I know. In addition to his business, Jerry was a philanthropist, a scholar, and a true humanitarian. Jerry Hahn had a positive influence on my later life.

During the twenty years they were married, Dorothy and Jerry Hahn had three sons: Jonathan, Ari, and Steven. Jonathan and Ari became Hassidic Jews and lived as if they were seventeenth-century, Eastern European, ultra-orthodox Jews. Their children and grandchildren have continued the same observant life.

My sister Dorothy is now the mother, grandmother, and great grandmother of at least sixty boys and girls.

In May 1951, President Harry Truman fired General of the Army Douglas MacArthur for insubordination.

In the summer of 1951, I was seventeen years old. By then, 2,900,000 American soldiers were fighting in Korea. (At eighteen, I had a student deferment and was exempt from the draft until 1956.)

I applied to several colleges and universities, including Lehigh and Princeton. My best friend at the time, Ted Glatzer, lived around the corner from me in on Avon Road in Jamaica Estates. Ted had an older brother Seymour, who had graduated from Lehigh seven years earlier. I was accepted at Lehigh, but sadly, Ted was not.

At about the same time, Princeton wrote me that they could not admit me for the September semester but if there were any openings for the spring semester, they would let me know. I started my college career at Lehigh hoping to transfer to Princeton the following February—but that is another story.

I had planned with two other friends to, upon graduation from Jamaica High School in the summer of 1951, take a railroad trip to California. The plan was to take the northern route outbound and the southern route home. When it came time to plan the itinerary and purchase the rail tickets, the other boys' parents said no. I was determined to take the trip on my own.

Although I was not yet eighteen, my parents fully supported my plan to travel alone, by railroad, across the entire United States for six weeks. Arrangements were made for various parental friends to put me up in their homes while visiting the cities where they lived.

My first stop was Chicago, where I stayed at the home of our Fuller Tool sales representative, Sammy Peachin and his wife Blossom. Sammy took me to a Chicago Turkish bath for a full-body massage by a huge, bald Turk.

On the way west, I stayed a few days in Yellowstone Park and Sun Valley, and saw a rodeo in Pocatello, Idaho. Traveling through the Grand Tetons, I sat in a glass-top rail car, which provided a magnificent view of the snow-covered peaks.

In Seattle, I stayed with Julius and Freddie Myers and their three kids. The Meyers kept a speedboat on Lake Washington.

Their kids, then aged five, seven, and eleven, persuaded me to take them out in the boat. At seventeen, they thought I must know how to drive a speedboat. They soon realized that they were far more capable than I was.

From Seattle, I rode a Greyhound bus to Portland, Oregon. A new experience soon awaited me. My hotel reservation somehow got lost and, because there was a convention in town, my only option was the local YMCA. For two dollars, I was given a bunk bed in a large dormitory. That night, ten or twelve drunks playing dice and card games until sunup kept me awake. The good news is I enjoyed the best salmon dinner I have ever had.

The Worby family, originally from Laurelton, were my hosts in Los Angeles. We toured the big movie studios, and they took me around the Knott's Berry Farm. Walt Disney had not yet built Disney Land.

In the southwest, I spent time exploring the Grand Canyon from the back of a surefooted mule. In Colorado, I took a scary bus ride to the summit of Pikes Peak (highest mountain on the mainland) and became sick from the lack of oxygen.

I engaged with anyone and everyone, from American Indian locals to tourists.

On the train ride back to Chicago, someone in the club car started a collection for me and raised almost fifty dollars.

I struck up a conversation with an older couple from Highland Park, Illinois, a wealthy suburb of Chicago. After a while, they invited me to stay with them at their home. They invited me to play golf at their club. I accepted and it was a great weekend.

In early August, I took a flight home from Chicago to LaGuardia Airport on a Capital Airlines DC-3.

Traveling alone, across the United States as a boy showed me that most Americans are generous, very friendly, and courteous. I also learned that America is a *big country*.

Chapter 6
Lehigh University

September 1951:

In that year, the first commercial computer, UNIVAC1, started government service. *I Love Lucy* debuted on television. Milton Berle was on television on Tuesday nights.

In my two-door 1950 Dodge, I drove to Bethlehem, Pennsylvania to start my first semester at Lehigh. My dorm was Dravo Hall, named for a Lehigh alumnus who made it big in the steel industry fifty years earlier and contributed money to the university.

The most singular recollection I have of the first few weeks was the unpleasant odor of sulphuric acid coming from the Bethlehem Steel factory overlooking the grimy little city.

My other memory was of meeting up with the few Jewish boys. (No women were admitted to Lehigh until years later.) However, the first black student ever admitted to Lehigh was in my class.

I soon struck up a friendship with Steve Gutman, who graduated from Bronx High School of Science, and Andy Jeffrey, who graduated from Great Neck High School. We would all remain lifelong friends.

Freshmen—even the Jewish kids—were required to attend the Episcopal chapel every Sunday morning. The Lehigh campus is extremely hilly, and it seemed like every class was held in a different building. The chapel was at the very bottom of the large campus.

Although there was a Jewish fraternity, Sigma Alpha Mu or "Sammy," and a Hillel group, the relatively few Jewish students were not made especially welcome. My friends and I had grown up in Great Neck, Jamica Estates, the Bronx, and Brooklyn. We were unaccustomed to close association with Gentile boys. Lehigh was a culture shock.

Every weekend at every fraternity, there was a lot of drinking and partying. The movie *House Party* could have been based on a typical weekend at Lehigh University.

Snyder's (semi-kosher) delicatessen became my favorite eatery. You could buy two slices of corned beef on rye for fifty cents.

On most Saturdays, we attended Lehigh football games. The star quarterback was a "Sammy." The Lehigh wrestling team led in its division. Steve Gutman, Andy Jeffrey, and I hung out together, got drunk together, and even at times studied together.

In the first semester, we attended classes, trudged up and down steep hills, endured dismal weather, and ate bad food. We indulged in too many five-cent candy bars and drank too much cheap alcohol. With no girls around, there were few social opportunities. I was anxious to come home for Thanksgiving.

A surprise awaited me. My mother said a letter had come from Princeton that said I was accepted for the spring semester.

"Wow. That's great. Show me the letter," I said.

Her reply was, "It's gone. I threw it in the garbage. If they didn't want you before, you don't need them now."

From then on, the relationship with my mother changed, but not for the better.

Don't misunderstand. I believe my life and career has worked out wonderfully. I would not have met Pat or had my wonderful children, David and Susan.

On returning to Lehigh, I put aside my disappointment and resumed my studies. Fraternity life was not my thing, so I traveled with a few other boys (Steve Gutman, Andy Jeffrey, Jerry Unger, and Pete Levine) to nearby Centenary College for Women and had a pretty good time after all.

The summer following my freshman year, my roommate Andy Jeffrey gave a party at his home in Great Neck. He invited me and his college buddies, including Steve and Jerry Unger, a redhead like me.

Andy asked Pat Green, his (platonic) friend from Great Neck High, if she would act as his party hostess.

Pat was a student at Simmons College, a women's college in Boston. The way I remember it, Pat and I got into a long conversation and I told her I would call her soon.

A few days later, I called Pat and identified myself as the "redhead she met at Andy's party." I invited her for a ride in my mother's Oldsmobile convertible. Pat greeted me at the door at 7 Linden with a puzzled look on her face.

"You're not the redhead I expected," she said.

Turns out, Pat thought she had made a date with Jerry Unger, the other redhead at Andy's party, but it was too late to back out. We went for a spin in my mother's car. I was smitten. Pat, not so much.

At the time, I was one week shy of my nineteenth birthday. Up to then, I had dated a few girls in high school and "played the field" during college.

Most of the girls I met were not interested or knowledgeable in things that interested me.

I had read everything about the new state of Israel and had spent a summer at a kibbutz camp. I had studied both piano and violin and enjoyed classical music. On Broadway, I had seen *Oklahoma*, *Carousel*, and Jimmy Cagney as George M. Cohan. Art books at home were well worn. Golf was already my favorite sport. I had been on the swim team at Jamaica High and president of Young Judea.

Before college, I had traveled the United States on my own and visited Havana, Cuba before Castro.

Pat Green was interesting and from a far less religious family than my own. Plus, I found her very attractive.

I was stricken from the beginning. She was not. It would take another four years of getting together and a few long breakups before I convinced her that we were meant to be together for the rest of our lives.

During second semester, Steve Gutman, Andy Jeffrey, and I rented the top floor of an old three-story house in Bethlehem. A couple things about that house remain in my memory.

We found some used dormitory furniture and hauled it up three flights to the apartment. The couch, however, wouldn't fit through the front door. We rigged up a pulley to pull it up from outside and through a large living room window.

Steve was a "neat nick," but I was not. Andy was the worst. Steve did the cooking and cleaning, as he was the only one who cared.

During spring break 1953, Pat came down from Boston for a weekend at Lehigh. I don't remember much else.

After two years at Lehigh, Steve transferred to New York University to be near his ailing mother. Andy dropped out and joined the army. They sent him to Korea.

With my two best friends no longer at Lehigh, I decided to transfer to Hofstra on Long Island. I could live at home until graduation. After that, I would start work as a traveling salesman for my father's company.

Meanwhile, Pat was still at Simmons College in Boston, and we had not seen each other for some time. When I got back from Lehigh, I dated a few girls and went to temple dances at the Forest Hills Jewish Center and Hillcrest Jewish Center.

In those days, most girls didn't go to college, but were looking to marry a guy with a good job, a car, and maybe a little money. I would compare every girl I met to Pat and none of them measured up. I got the brush off every time I called her, but I kept trying.

Pat finally said, "Ask me again after you graduate college. But we are not engaged." I took that as a hopeful sign.

Pat's folks belonged to Glen Oaks Country Club, which my parents had also recently joined. I had a summer job at Strauss Auto Store. After work, I would drive to Great Neck just in time for appetizers and dinner with Pat and her family. It was 1953: the best summer ever.

In the spring of 1954, the Supreme Court outlawed school segregation in the landmark case of *Brown v. Board of Education*, argued and won by Thurgood Marshall.

In June 1954, Joseph Welch said to Senator Joe McCarthy, "At long last, have you no sense of decency?" That was the end of McCarthy's Senate career.

Over the next two years (September 1953 to June 1955), I worked hard to earn a BA degree in business administration at Hofstra College (now Hofstra University).

My best friend from high school, Joel Gitlin, lived in a big Tudor-style house high above Midland Parkway. Every morning, I would bound up the forty-two steps to the front door and head directly to their refrigerator.

Joel had an older sister, Hope, and a younger sister named Grace. Hope Gitlin had recently contracted a life-threatening neurological disease that left her totally blind at twenty-three years of age. Hope was also a student at Hofstra College. Each day, I would drive her to Hofstra and lead her by her arm to her first class. Other friends would guide her from there. After classes, I would drive her home. Never once did she complain about suddenly losing her sight. One year later, Hope died.

One spring day, Joel asked me if I wanted to attend a violin recital that his mother was hosting in their home. I had studied the violin as a kid and I was thrilled to attend. There were about thirty women seated on folding chairs in their large living room with two grand pianos. A very young, short, chubby man about twenty-two years old, played for over an hour. It was amazing. At the time, Isaac Stern was unknown. He had not yet performed at Carnegie Hall, although years later he raised enough money to save the hall from demolition.

Chapter 7
My Wife, Pat Green

The story of Pat's biological father, Harold Davis, is long lost. However, a few details were shared with me.

Harold Isador Davis was born in Erie, Pennsylvania in February 1893. The family lived at 212 West Fourth Street in Erie, Pennsylvania. Harold's sister Belle was older, born about 1890.

Their parents were Joseph and Dora Davis. Grandpa Joseph was born in Cleveland around 1865, as was Grandma Dora in Toronto, Canada. Pat's paternal ancestors arrived from Germany or possibly Austria during the second great period of German Jewish immigration (between 1849 and 1880).

During World War 1, Harold Davis was stationed at Fort Lewis in Tacoma, Washington. Harold's mother Dora was born in Toronto and knew the Vise family. When Harold returned east after the war, Dora introduced her son Harold to Etta Vise. Etta was probably eighteen years old and Harold was ten years older.

Basically, it was an arranged marriage. After the wedding, Harold returned to Tacoma, Washington. They bought a comfortable house at 920 North Tacoma Avenue. Harold opened an insurance brokerage. In 1931, their daughter Jo was born, followed in 1934 by Patricia (Pat) Davis.

There was a small Jewish community in Tacoma at that time and Harold Davis served as president of the temple.

In the 1930s and 40s, Gig Island was mostly farmland and not far from Tacoma. Pat's family owned a farm on the island run by a tenant farmer. On summer weekends, Pat and her sister Jo enjoyed swimming in the lake, chasing chickens, and milking cows.

The island is located directly below the Tacoma Narrows Bridge, known locally as "Galloping Gertie." In November 1940, just five months after it was completed, the bridge was hit by a strong gust of wind and collapsed into Puget Sound.

Sometime during 1942, Harold developed a heart condition. Etta could do little for her husband. He was sick at home for two years before he died in 1944 at age fifty-one. Jo was twelve and Pat was nine.

Etta and the two girls returned to Toronto, where Etta had been born and had many family members. When the war was finally over in 1945, Etta and the two girls moved to New York City. They lived at the Croyden Hotel.

Etta had met Jerry Green when Jerry's father was a patient at Mt. Sinai Hospital in New York, where Etta was a nurse. It was 1946 and Etta was a widow. Jerry Green had never married.

Through a mutual friend, Etta and Jerry renewed their friendship. Not long after, they were married in the Sutton Place apartment of Barney and Rose Robinson.

Jerry and Etta built their new home at 7 Linden Boulevard in Great Neck. This is where I met Pat in the summer of 1951.

The Green family enjoyed a lifestyle that was new to me. Pat's parents were very generous, welcoming, and fun loving.

Every day during the summer of 1951 was memorable. I was invited several times to play golf at (the old) Glen Oaks Club with Dr. Green.

Jerry Green was a forty-seven-year-old orthodontist. Pat's mom Etta Vise Green was now a widow with two young girls. They enjoyed a wonderful life with many friends and family, both his and hers. They included me for Sunday barbecues, holidays, and social events at Glen Oaks Country Club.

Their home was comfortable, relaxed, and welcoming, not at all like what I had come from.

Instead of my own mother's overcooked or undercooked chicken, I now enjoyed a glass of Scotch and a shrimp cocktail on the patio, followed by a two-inch porterhouse steak, grilled very rare on a charcoal fire, with ice cream and homemade apple pie for dessert.

Chapter 8
A Traveling Salesman

Finally, on a Friday morning in June 1955, I graduated from Hofstra College with a bachelor's degree in business administration.

On the following Monday, my business career began in earnest with a series of two week-long sales trips visiting hardware wholesalers in New England, New York state, Pennsylvania, and west to Ohio and Indiana. My territory covered the length of the Mississippi River from Minneapolis to Orleans. I travelled mostly by car, but long trips were on a low and slow DC-3.

I did not know it at the time, but those first sales trips were like earning a master's degree from Harvard Business School. I had to convince customers that Fuller screwdrivers with unbreakable plastic handles would sell better than traditional screwdrivers with wooden handles that could easily break.

With a brief case full or hand tool orders, I returned to the office in the Bronx. When I got there, everyone was busy with his or her own issues and paid no attention to me. "I got orders." I shouted to no one

In particular, "Give them to Kal," someone said, and that was that. No kudos, no "Atta Boy," just, "Give them to Kal."

I quickly realized that my job as a company salesman was to visit as many customers as I could and not to leave a buyer's office without an order. I was a traveling salesman. I made my own schedule, booked my hotels, and made appointments with buyers. My boss was Johnny Weil, not Bernie Fuller.

In addition to selling Fuller Tools, I also sold Fuller's steak knives and carving sets until my brother-in-law Jerry Hahn created Regent Sheffied Ltd.

On one sales trip, I had an appointment with the buyer of a well-known five- and ten-cent store chain called G.C. Murphy Company. They were a good customer of Fuller tools but had never purchased Fuller cutlery. I showed the buyer a sample of our three-piece carving set.

The buyer took the ten-inch carving knife from me and as I watched, stood the knife on its tip and bore down. The blade bent at a forty-five-degree angle to the handle. Suddenly, the thin blade came out of its handle and was on the floor.

I was so taken aback that I said to the buyer, "You broke my only sample. Now I have nothing to sell."

His reply was straight to the point: "This is crap and you shouldn't be selling it." As he was a lot older than me and a long-time customer, I had to agree with him.

When I got back to the office, I told Jerry Hahn about the broken carving knife. Jerry did not seem surprised. He had been unhappy with the quality of Fuller cutlery for a long time and had made the decision to only use forged steel, not cheap, stamped steel blades. Jerry was determined to separate the cutlery operation from Fuller Tool Company and had decided the company would be called Regent Sheffield Ltd.

After graduating from college in 1955 but before I was drafted into the US army (in which I served from February 1957 to January 1958), I was a traveling salesman for Fuller Tools and Cutlery. I enjoyed it and even got pretty good at it.

I had been around the factory floor since I was six years old and observed where bottlenecks slowed up production but was not shy about offering solutions. As the boss's son, it was easy for me to implement my ideas without anyone objecting.

Experience as a traveling salesman, working in the factory, plus a degree in business administration gave me confidence in my ability to become a businessman. Meanwhile, other life-altering events were on the horizon.

When traveling for Fuller Tool Company, I often had to spend many weekends away from home. I kept an old set of golf clubs in the trunk of my car in case there was a public golf course nearby.

On a two-week trip through the south, I arranged to spend the weekend at Pinehurst, a golfing destination in North Carolina. I stayed in a motel next to Pinehurst 2, a world-famous golf course that was open to the public.

On Saturday morning, I went to the coffee shop for breakfast, hoping to meet some other guys that I could play golf with. As luck would have it, I spotted a table of three men.

I casually enquired if they needed a "fourth." They were very welcoming, and we were soon on the first tee. My old golf bag with about six clubs looked shabby and elicited comments that I might be a "ringer" (someone who carries a beat-up set of clubs, claims he can barely play the game, and by the end of the day, wins a lot of money).

In the morning round, we walked eighteen holes (electric golf carts had not yet been invented). After lunch, we switched partners and played another eighteen holes before retiring to the "nineteenth" hole. I was invited to join them for drinks and a steak dinner, which I gladly accepted.

Afterward, one of the men, a young doctor from Westchester by the name of Shep, took me aside and questioned me very closely. What company did I work for? Did I graduate from college? Where did I live? Did I have a girlfriend? (Yes.) I wondered why all the questions but soon found out.

Shep said, "I just spent an entire day playing golf with you, and golf is a great way to learn about a person. My father-in-law, Barney Robinson, plays golf at Glen Oaks Club in Great Neck with his friend, Jerry Green. I think you would like Jerry's daughter, Pat. If interested, I could get you Pat's phone number."

I said, "Thanks Shep, but since Pat Green and I are already engaged, I already have her phone number." That is a true story.

Pat and I became engaged to be married in the summer of 1956. Pat's folks hosted an engagement party on the lawn at 7 Linden.

It was a wonderful party. Etta told my mother how happy she was that 'the kids are getting married." Helen Fuller replied, "They are only engaged. Who said anything about marriage?" This, of course, stunned Pat's mother.

Dr. Green had been a member of the prestigious Glen Oaks Country Club since 1925 and was a Class A golf champion.

Helen Fuller would have preferred I married into a more "middle class" family, like the family of Irving and Viola Hahn. Their son Jerry married my sister Dorothy.

Helen Fuller was cold and distant to my future family, which would in time bring Pat's mother Etta to tears.

Chapter 9
My Lovable Uncle Marty (Dad's Older Brother)

During the winter of 1956, my sister Dee was vacationing with her husband Jerry Hahn at the Fontainebleau Hotel in Miami Beach.

Dee began chatting with the woman on the chaise next to hers.

The woman was from Detroit and said her last name was Fuller. My sister told her that Fuller was her maiden name.

"What is your husband's first name?" my sister asked.

"Marty," the woman answered.

"Now isn't that something. I have an uncle, Marty Fuller from New York, who frequently travels to Detroit on business." After a while, my sister enquired, "Do you have any children?"

"Oh yes, we have a son and a daughter."

"What does your husband do?" she asked.

"Marty is a prize fight manager and promoter," the other woman replied.

Dee was becoming unnerved. Was it possible that this woman from Detroit was married to the same Uncle Marty, her father's brother, who had a wife and two children in New York and was a prize fight manager?

It was too much to absorb.

As soon as she got home, Dee called our father and told him about meeting a Mrs. Fuller from Detroit, who was married to a man named Marty, a prize fight manager.

My father's sister Paula was the closest to Marty. My father said he would call Paula and relay Dee's story.

It turned out that Aunt Paula had known for a long time that Marty Fuller from Detroit was their beloved brother from New York. Marty had a wife and two children in New York and, at the same time, a different wife and two children in Detroit. All four of his children, two boys and two girls, were about the same ages.

The affair had been going on for at least ten years. His first wife in New York was my Aunt Kitty. Their two children, Judy and Harris, are my first cousins, as are the two children in Detroit.

We were all upset for Kitty and the kids. Marty immediately became persona non grata. Knowing that Uncle Marty was my favorite uncle, I was asked if I still wanted to invite Marty to my upcoming wedding. I said I did as his love life had nothing to do with me. Marty was invited, but never showed up.

Some years later, Pat and I had rented an apartment in Boca West, Florida for the winter. One day, while I was playing golf and Pat was at the pool, she struck up a conversation with a woman from Detroit.

The woman had married Uncle Marty's Detroit son. They had since divorced. Her former husband worked for Marty, selling Fuller tools in the Detroit area.

If Marty was selling Fuller tools in Detroit, it made sense that my father already knew that Marty had a wife and family in Detroit. That he probably always knew about it did not surprise me.

Another time while in London on business, I was invited by our English friends Ruth and Maurice Felber to meet them for dinner in London. They had also invited an American couple from Detroit.

Since the only person I knew in Detroit was my devious uncle, I casually asked if they knew a certain Marty Fuller.

Of course. They had once lived on the same street as Marty Fuller and his family and were friends with both of his children. They knew that Marty was a sometime fight manager who also sold hand tools.

I could not resist telling them the story of Marty Fuller in New York and Detroit. They were shocked and incredulous and could hardly wait to tell everyone back in Detroit.

Chapter 10
Marriage and the Military

One day in September 1956, I got a postcard from my draft board enquiring about my marital status. Was I single or married?

If I returned the card marked married, there was a chance I would be deferred. The Korean war had ended with an armistice. The only reason for a large standing army was to show Stalin and the Russians that America, as a member of NATO, would defend Western Europe.

Our First Wedding

To report to the draft board that I was married, on October 4, 1956, we were married by Judge Edwards of the Civil Court in Great Neck. Etta and Jerry Green, Pat, and I made up the entire wedding party.

As far as my mother was concerned, until a rabbi performed a proper Jewish ceremony under a chuppah, we were not really married. She insisted I return home that night, alone, and that Pat go home with her mother.

The "Religious" Wedding

Ten days later October 14, 1956, at the Roosevelt Hotel, we were married for the second time. Rabbi Israel Moshowitz officiated.

Burt Rockaway was my best man and the only one of my friends, or of Pat's friends, in attendance.

Traditionally, the bride's family pays for the wedding. My mother demanded strictly kosher food. The Greens complied but limited the guest list to family members and a few very close friends. Seventy-five people were invited and attended.

I don't remember much about the wedding except that Pat got the "giggles" while we were standing under the chuppah. Later, she said it just struck her funny that we were being married for the second time in two weeks.

The following day, Pat and I boarded a flight to San Francisco. We had to stop in Chicago as nonstop flights to the west coast were not yet possible. When we finally arrived at our hotel (The Mark), it was dinner time. We were both starving and headed for Chinatown. We went to a famous Chinese restaurant, ordered our food, and started drinking water. We were both so thirsty the waiter kept refilling our glasses. When the food finally came, we were so bloated with water that we couldn't eat a thing. We took our dinner back to our hotel.

On a side trip to Los Angeles to visit Disney Land, we stayed at the Hilton Hotel, where we literally bumped into President Eisenhower while he was campaigning for his second term with Vice President Richard Nixon.

From there, we flew to Las Vegas, Nevada. At that time, Las Vegas was quite small—nothing like it is today. The Strip was a few low-rise motels with huge neon signs advertising acts by Frank Sinatra, Jimmy Durante, Bob Hope, and, in the (free) lounge, Louis Prima and Keely Smith.

On our return to New York, we found a small apartment in Jamaica. It was in an old building near the subway station at Sutphin Boulevard—a far cry from Great Neck and Jamaica Estates. It was pretty crummy, but on my saleman's salary of one hundred dollars per week, it was all we could afford.

We lived there from October 1956 through January 1957, when my draft notice arrived. I was ordered to report to Whitehall Street within thirty days.

Chapter 11
The Military

"Greetings. You have been selected to report for induction into the United States Army, at 100 Whitehall Street at 8 a.m. February 5, 1957. Failure to report will result in your immediate arrest and trial." They were serious.

The first day as an inductee is super stressful. The world suddenly becomes a strange place, populated by uniformed men with guns. They tell you to take off your clothes, sit here, go there, wait in line, fill this out, and so on. Doctors poke you, take your temperature, check your eyes and your feet, and ask you a few questions to be sure you are not sick or homosexual. At the end of a long day, everyone assembles under an American flag and is required to pledge allegiance to the flag, the United States, and the commander in chief, President Eisenhower.

"Congratulations. You are now a member of the greatest military force in the world, the US Army."

By the time we left Whitehall Street, it was 7:00 p.m. We were loaded onto buses for a three-hour trip to Fort Dix in New Jersey. By the time we got to New Jersey, I only wanted to get off the bus and go home.

At that moment, it suddenly hit me that I had no *freedom*. I was in the army now.

At about 10:00 p.m., we arrived at a set of grey wooden buildings, lit by bright streetlights. I felt like a prisoner, which I was. After picking up an armful of bedding, including a thin mattress, we were marched, two by two, into the barracks, which would be our home for the next nine weeks.

Walking next to me was a skinny, nineteen-year-old Italian kid from Babylon, Long Island. His name was Nick DiPrima. As I was older (twenty-three), I grabbed the lower bunk. First, however, we had to make up our beds and get to sleep as quickly as possible.

The young sergeant assigned to our group (squad?) told us that reveille would sound at 5:00 a.m. sharp, and we would have fifteen minutes to wash, dress, and assemble on the parade grounds outside of our barracks. It was a very short night.

True to his word, a recorded bugle blasted over the loudspeaker at exactly 5:00 a.m. I noted with some satisfaction that the sergeant must have gotten up before us as he was in uniform and screaming at us to "get up and get going."

The first week in the army is called Zero Week. In other words, it doesn't count toward the regular eight weeks of basic training.

Zero week sounds innocent. The truth is the first week in the army can be traumatic for someone who has never spent time in police custody or lost his "free will." It's like being stuck in an elevator.

You have suddenly lost control of where you can go and what you can do. You are at the mercy of others. You quickly realize that there are no options, so you do as you are told. Only your thoughts are your own, nothing else, not even the clothes on your back. You belong to the US army.

During the first week, you are issued uniforms, have your hair cut off, suffer a series of vaccinations, have eye exams, and learn how to stand for hours in formation. You must learn the proper way to salute and who to salute. You are asked about any special aptitudes or skills you may have. You stand in line for something you never have seen much less eaten in your entire life. The guiding principle that every recruit understands from day one is "Hurry up and wait!"

At the end of Zero Week, we were permitted to go home for the weekend but God help those who don't get back to the barracks by 6:00 p.m. on Sunday night.

Basic training started at 5:00 a.m. every day for the next eight weeks. However, as a married couple, Pat and I were allowed to live off base during training. We found a place on the second floor of an old house in Bordentown, New Jersey, about fifteen minutes from Fort Dix. I had to be at Fort Dix by 6:00 a.m. every day.

Pat drove me to the base while listening to the morning farm reports. By then, I had traded in the old Dodge for a new 1956 Pontiac for $2,000. It had an automatic shift and big, whitewall tires.

A typical day of basic training during the initial eight weeks included four hours of classroom work and a break every hour. We sat through boring lectures covering military terminology, famous battles, and medals and what they signify. We learned military tactics and other information essential for soldiers.

Exams were pass or fail. If you failed, you might lose the weekend pass and spend the weekend scrubbing the barracks floor with a toothbrush.

If a coin did not briskly bounce off the blanket, your footlocker was messy, your shoes not shined, or you failed to salute correctly, you might not get your coveted weekend pass, while everyone else went home. It made us concentrate.

After basic training, we were sent by train to Fort Benning, Georgia for another eight weeks of field manuevers and real weapons training. At Fort Benning, the training became serious. We learned how to assemble and reassemble a World War 2 rifle weighing fifteen pounds in under two minutes. We learned how to throw a hand grenade from a foxhole without blowing up our trainer or ourselves. We learned how to crawl under barbed wire with live bullets only two feet over our heads.

Every day, we ran five miles with full packs and a twelve-pound rifle before breakfast. We marched ten miles after lunch. I still remember riding in the back of an open truck, and using my steel helmet as a pillow.

At the end of a grueling nine weeks, we received our new orders. I could have been assigned to an infantry unit (the worst), the Tank Corps, or the Artillery.

What I hoped for was the job of company clerk. This required typing, but I didn't know how to type.

In 1957 in Columbus, Georgia, Jim Crow laws forced the separation of black people from others. The Ku Klux Klan was very active in the area and made sure the separation was enforced. The Supreme Court had not yet struck down the doctrine of "separate but equal." When I was there, it was against the law for a black soldier to be on the streets of Columbus, Georgia after dark. In February, that was 5:00 p.m.

The city authorities even enforced anti-miscegenation (racial intermarriage) and other restrictive Jim Crow laws. Federal law could supersede, but that never happened, at least not in 1957. Black soldiers were restricted to certain areas of town, and had their own movie theater, food stores, and drinking fountains. As a kid from New York, it seemed unfair, and we all felt bad for our fellow soldiers.

There was nothing we could do or say. Jews weren't exactly welcome either. It was the deepest of the Deep South. The Civil war had ended 103 years before, but it didn't feel like it.

The civil rights movement was in its earliest stages. The Montgomery bus strike and a few lunch counter incidents had occurred. Martin Luther King was still a preacher at the Ebenezer Baptist Church in Atlanta when I was training at Fort Benning, Georgia.

At last. Basic training was over. It was the third week of April 1957.

We assembled on the parade ground and marched past the commanding generals as soldiers of the armed forces of the United States of America. We were a fighting machine.

Most of my buddies were sent to Korea or Japan, and some to England and Germany. Japan and Germany were no longer occupied countries but did host US military forces as a part of NATO.

The Soviet Union controlled East Germany and all of Eastern Europe. In 1957, there were still two million US troops scattered around the world.

My new assignment was posted on the barracks bulletin board. I could hardly believe my good luck! My college education would pay off. For the next four weeks, I was ordered to attend IBM school on Park Avenue in Manhattan. Nick D' Prima, my bunkmate was assigned to an infantry battalion at Fort Hood, Texas. If war broke out, he would be on the front lines.

At IBM school, I learned to type forty words per minute on an IBM typewriter. Once I mastered that, I learned to operate a key punch machine. Meanwhile, Pat and I stayed in the guest room at 7 Linden in Great Neck. I caught the Long Island Railroad at 8:05, wore civilian clothes, and played golf with Jerry Green on the weekends. My army pay was ninety dollars per week.

After completing IBM school, I was assigned to the Pentagon in Washington, DC. Our unit was responsible for the daily count of every soldier in the US army, wherever they were in the world. My supervisor was another draftee, Corporal Howie Maidenbaum, from Roslyn, New York, a village two miles from Great Neck.

We toiled in a temperature-controlled room the size of a football field, five floors underground. In the center of the room was Eniac, the most powerful computer in the world. My unit was MRU 1 (Machine Records Unit 1). The work was mind numbing, but it would not be my last military posting.

Working at the Pentagon for eight hours a day, we entered numbers on large sheets of paper into a bulky machine with keys that punched holes in a computer card. It was not unlike a Braille machine. Every 100 cards were bundled, marked, and passed on to the supervisor. The cards were then loaded into a giant sorting machine and dropped into hundreds of different slots. From there, the information was transferred to tape.

Entering numbers in a key punch machine was mindless and endless.

During our lunch breaks, we would smoke and talk with our friends in a small park at the center of the Pentagon

Key punchers do not stay long. After a few months, carpal tunnel syndrome and boredom can cause errors. There were plenty of fresh recruits eager to work in the basement of the Pentagon.

After six months, we were informed that new orders would soon come down. If they sent me overseas, which seemed likely, Pat would not be able to join me.

Meanwhile, we had rented a small apartment in Arlington, Virginia. We shopped at the army PX. The PX sold everything from groceries to appliances, clothes, liquor, gasoline, and anything else you might need or want. Prices were 40 percent lower than regular retail prices. Looking back, the PX was Walmart before Walmart!

Our apartment in Arlington was about twenty minutes from the Pentagon. On most days, Pat would drive me to work and pick me up at 4:00 p.m.

One day, Pat decided she would make a top round of beef for dinner. After coming home, she prepared the meat and put it in the oven for four hours. At dinnertime, she didn't feel well. She said the roast was done and I should have some for my dinner.

I did as instructed and after dinner, Pat asked me how the roast was. "Well," I said, "it wasn't as tender as your mother's, but it was good."

The next night, Pat warmed up the roast and cut some slices for both of us. After just one bite, Pat looked at me aghast. "How did you eat this? It's so tough I cannot chew it."

It seems that top round must be cooked for ten hours, not four hours. I wasn't going to complain about her cooking skills. I just chewed it longer than usual. Hey, I was hungry.

We enjoyed Washington, DC and became friendly with two other couples from Long Island: Howie and Eppie Maidenbaum and Ronald and Barbara Mandler.

I had known Ron Mandler from Hofstra. During college, he was dating Barbara, and they were married about the same month and year as us. For many years, even after Ron and Howie died, we maintained our friendships.

Finally, new orders came down. I was reassigned to 7th Army headquarters, Stuttgart, Germany. There was no war in progress and married soldiers could live together off base. Pat could come with me. It was going to be an exciting new chapter in our lives, and a welcome change from my key punch job in the basement of the Pentagon.

If you worked at the Pentagon, the US Army Travel office booked all travel to Europe via military air transport (MATS). I traveled on a converted B-24 Air Force bomber that made several refueling stops before its final stop in Greenland. We were warned not to touch the metal step railing as our hands would freeze to the metal.

Basic Training, 1957, Fort Benning, Georgia

Chapter 12
Stuttgart, Germany; Kenny and Robert Lonoff

The first few days in Germany were spent processing and getting acquainted with the other soldiers, officers, and non-commissioned officers who would control my life for the next twelve months.

My rank was still that of private—not private first class (PFC), just plain private. It would take twenty months for me to reach PFC.

Pat was due to arrive in a few days, on a TWA flight from Idlewild International Airport on one of the first 747 jet airplanes. At that time, only TWA flew the new 747 Luxury Airliner. While I waited for the plane to land, I struck up a conversation with another fellow who was also waiting for his wife. We were both in civilian clothes, so I did not realize he was an officer. He did not know I was an enlisted man, a draftee, and worse, a lowly private.

Had we both been in uniform, he told me later, he would not have struck up a conversation. As it happens, we were both waiting for the same flight and got to talking. Lt. Lonoff told me he had gone through the ROTC program at Bucknell University. I told him I had gone to Lehigh University and left him with the impression that I, too, was an ROTC officer.

The flight was about an hour late, and in that hour, Kenny Lonoff and I forged a lifelong friendship. We were two guys from the New York area, stationed in the same country that had recently killed six million Jews. Still, we had to live and work alongside former Nazis.

When their plane landed, Roberta Lonoff walked down the first-class steps in the front of the 747. Ten minutes later, I spotted Pat coming out of the tourist section. My father had paid for her flight (as did Birdie's father). Roberta and Pat hit it off right away.

We promised to call them in a few days to get together. They were staying at the officer's club in Stuttgart and gave us the telephone number of the front desk. "Just ask for Lt. Lonoff," they told us. "It's easy to remember our name. Just think of on-off."

In a few days, we called the officer's club at the number they had given us, but there was no one there by that name. We kept trying, but no one by that name was registered.

One day, we ran into Birdie and Ken at the PX.

"Why didn't you call?" they asked. We told them we did call the officer's club several times.

"Did you ask for Lt. Lonoff, as in on-off?"

"Oh. We thought it rhymed with in-out and asked for Lt. Linout."

As you might have guessed, the "Linout" story has been told many times over our sixty years of friendship.

Although we were stationed on different military bases and lived in different towns, we would get together with Kenny and Roberta as much as possible.

One Sunday, we fired up our PX bar-b-que grill on the terrace of our tenth-floor apartment to grill some steaks for the Lonoffs. Naturally, there was a lot of smoke. Suddenly, the local fire department was banging on our door. Our neighbor thought our apartment was on fire.

I needed a car to get back and forth from our apartment in Stuttgart to the army base in Viangen, about five miles outside of town. I found a five-year-old Mercedes-Benz with a stick shift and a sunroof.

As a lowly, married private, my pay was a lofty $120 per month. My father, on behalf of his employee who had been drafted to serve for two years, agreed to supplement my income. We rented an apartment in downtown Stuttgart. The building, at 1 Stitsinberg Plaza, had been built after the war. It was quite nice and had a balcony where we kept a charcoal grill.

During the day, Pat shopped on the economy, and in so doing, learned to speak some German, for example, one day, she decided to make some coleslaw. Not knowing the word for coleslaw, she pointed to a nice head of cabbage. The grocer said, "Fraulein, das ist kraut." That's how she learned to speak German.

Meanhile, on the base, my first assignment was to mop the floor and clean the office toilets. Every newcomer got that job until the next guy was assigned to Headquarters Company.

However, the army had not sent me to IBM school to learn how to mop floors. My next assignment was as company librarian, army speak for "file clerk."

Chapter 13
Bill Ferriter

On the job, I met Bill Ferriter. He seemed a lost soul, so I invited him over to our apartment for dinner. Pat liked him right away. Bill is a couple of years younger than me and is from San Francisco. He had dropped out of San Francisco State. His father was a criminal defense attorney and had defended one of the most notorious members of the Al Capone gang, "Baby Face" Nelson, a Las Vegas mobster and a known hit man.

Bill was nothing like his father. He was laid back, good looking, and blond haired with a talent for drawing, acting, and attracting women. He would walk around our small apartment quoting Dylan Thomas and Shakespeare.

On our own time while at work, Bill and I published a unit newsletter complete with political cartoons drawn by Bill. We covered the weekly happenings in HQ Company, and other items such as the Friday night movie schedule.

We covered promotions, transfers, and court-martials. Unfortunately, we failed to maintain "military correctness." After a few unflattering cartoons depicting higher ups and critical comments, we were summarily shut down. It was fun while it lasted.

After twenty months, I was promoted to private first class. The promotion came with a raise of twenty dollars per month and a better job.

I was assigned to the general staff, not to plan military tactics but to write short speeches when a general presented a soldier with a medal for some noteworthy act. His speech could not exceed one hundred words and had to follow a specific formula. My job was to fill in the blanks and then add a personal note to make the general look like he knew the heroic soldier. As far as I was concerned, any job in the army that did not require raking leaves, marching, or firing a weapon was a good army job.

Just Between Us

A few German civilians were employed by the army. In our office, a young German woman worked as an assistant to one of the officers. Her name was Svantia. Bill and Svantia began to see each other off base and on weekends. Through his German girlfriend, we met other young Germans. We did not talk about the recent war, Adolf Hitler, or the Holocaust.

One day, Bill came to me in a state of near panic. He told me that Svantia was pregnant. It was a serious offense if a US soldier had relations with a German woman. If the woman got pregnant, it would mean a court martial and a dishonorable discharge. Could I help facilitate an abortion for Svantia? Without concern for the outcome if it did not go well, or if Svantia changed her mind, I went all out for my friend Bill.

Bill Ferriter and Pat Fuller circa 1975

Back to Bill Ferriter…

I knew that Burt Rockaway, my high school buddy, had gone to medical school in Zurich, Switzerland before dropping out and Burt not only provided the name and address of a doctor, he also made an appointment for Svantia the following week.

The outcome was as had been hoped for. Svantia took a week off and returned to our unit as if nothing had happened. Bill was safe.

Traveling Europe with "General" Jerry Green

Pat's father was an orthodontist, and his patients were almost all young kids. In Great Neck, New York, when school is out for the summer, it's vacation time!

We had saved up our leave to travel around Europe with Pat's folks, Jerry and Etta Green, for two weeks in July 1958. I had the little Mercedes tuned up and ready to handle the high-speed autobahn.

While driving east toward Austria on the autobahn, we wanted to stop for lunch. Ahead of us was a US army officer's club and dining room. As an enlisted man, I would be denied access, as would any civilians.

Walking ahead of my father-in-law, I approached the sergeant stationed at the entrance to the officer's club. I was in civilian clothes because I was traveling on the "economy." I showed my army ID.

"Sergeant," I said, "I am aide to General Jerome Green, who is traveling with his wife and daughter." With a smart salute to "General" Green, the sergeant held the door open for our group.

We were promptly seated and approached by our German waiter. He asked if we would like an aperitif before ordering lunch. "Ja." Good idea. Pat and her mother ordered a glass of white wine. I ordered a Coca Cola and "General" Green ordered dry martini.

In a few minutes, drinks were served, except the waiter had misunderstood the order. In front of the "general," he carefully set down three large martinis.

He asked the waiter, "What is this? I ordered a dry martini. You have given me three martinis."

"Ah, no sir, I wrote down your order and clearly you ordered drei martini." The word *drei* is German for three. The waiter brought three dry martinis, as requested.

"No problem," the "general" said. "Leave them here."

We soon continued our way and arrived that evening in Vienna, where we stayed for two days. The Russians had occupied Vienna since the end of the war twelve years before and had only recently left. We were able to enjoy sachertortes, the opera, and Strauss music everywhere.

From Vienna, we headed to Salzburg, Mozart's birthplace. We had the good fortune to be there during the Mozart Summer Festival. Then, it was on to the Italian Alps into northern Italy.

We spent a weekend at the world-famous resort Villa D'Este on Lake Como. The views, the music, and the food were all fantastic. We were in a different world from the US army.

From Lake Como in the north, we drove south to Venice. Our hotel, located on the Grand Canal, was three hundred years old.

Our room was the favorite of George Sand, the famous female author, who preferred to dress in men's clothes. Sand was the traveling companion of Frédéric Chopin. Our room (and theirs) overlooked the Bridge of Sighs and the gondolas floating leisurely beneath us.

During a tour of a Venetian glass factory, Pat's folks purchased an eight-foot tall handmade "clown lamp." The lamp consisted of various arms, legs, and heads that were separate and had to be reassembled when and if the lamp arrived in Great Neck. It did get there but when finished, it was too tall for their living room.

On the nearby beach, we spied Perry Como, surrounded by a small crowd of young Italian girls. He was trying to enjoy an ice cream cone while signing autographs. In 1959, Perry Como was as popular as Frank Sinatra, and was heard on every continent. At that moment, he was an American tourist just trying to enjoy a melting ice cream cone. He did give us his autograph.

By the time we got back to Stuttgart, we had logged two thousand miles. The little car only broke down once. It had been a fantastic trip and much more fun than you would expect when traveling for two weeks with your in-laws. I would never have imagined that four members of the same family would enjoy traveling together for two weeks without dissension. That was a revelation.

A surprise awaited me when I returned to base. It seems that while I was away, the Inspector General (IG) had made a visit to my unit. On reviewing the company files, the IG found them in violation of army regulations. As a result, I was told to report to headquarters for a new assignment. A new job could mean sweeping leaves from the commanding general's front lawn.

As with almost every experience I had during my army service, my new job turned out to be far better than the job I had lost. My file indicated that I had put out a unit "paper." To the army, this showed that I was at least good at writing. I was offered the job of writing ceremonial speeches for an officer when bestowing a medal of any kind on a soldier. The job required some creative writing skills to make it seem like a big deal.

My new job gave me plenty of free time. When an opening came up on the company golf team, I tried out and won a place. That was fun.

The end of my time in Europe was fast approaching. It was time to close the apartment and for Pat to return to the States. I would follow a couple of weeks later, courtesy of the US Army.

The question was whether I would travel home on a slow military vessel (ten days of rough seas, bunk beds, and bad food) or could get a coveted spot on a MATS.

All returning soldiers had to be interviewed by an officer in order to fill out the proper papers. That person alone would decide who would go home by plane and who would go by ship. This would be a very important interview.

When the time came to be interviewed, I sat in a chair next to the second lieutenant's desk. He pulled my file and started to look at it when his phone rang. To prevent me from overhearing, he turned away from me with his left hand resting on the desk, maybe six inches from my face. I noticed a large college graduation ring. I could easily see his alma mater. Lt. Goldman had graduated from Bucknell, class of 1956. He probably knew my army friend, Lt. Kenny Lonoff.

When the phone call ended, he turned back to face me. At that moment, I looked at him very seriously and said, "You look familiar to me. Did you by any chance go to Bucknell University?"

"Yes," he replied.

I said, "Do you know Kenny Lonoff from Bucknell?"

"Kenny Lonoff? Of course. He was my fraternity brother at Bucknell."

I instantly made up the following story. "I sat with Kenny at a football game between Bucknell and Lehigh. After the game, Ken invited me back to his fraternity house. That's where I know you from. Do you know that Kenny and his wife Roberta are stationed here in Stuttgart? I have his phone number if you want to call him."

Of course, I did not meet Kenny and Roberta until arriving in Germany and the story about knowing him from Bucknell was not true.

The travel officer said, "Okay, I see you are scheduled back to the States."

Right there, he cut official orders for me to fly home first class, which is usually reserved for high-ranking officers.

The moral: when you see an opportunity, seize the moment.

My two years in the army were over. It was peacetime, with only a skirmish in Lebanon when everyone was put on high alert. We were able to experience a large part of Europe. We enjoyed meeting more people than we could imagine. Above all, we proved to ourselves that we could function successfully, even in an environment defined by rank. We could work with people of all races, religions, political beliefs, and those who spoke languages we didn't understand. Childhood, high school, college and the army were behind me. Now I had a wife to support. In January 1960, I turned twenty-four and was ready for anything—or so I thought.

By the way...

One of the best things the army taught me was the value of PT, i.e, physical training. When I returned to civilian life, I continued my daily workouts at home.

In the 1980s, many local gyms, patronized by amateur fighters, converted to co-ed membership clubs to attract anyone who just wanted to lose a few pounds.

The first PT club I joined was in the Miracle Mile in Manhasset, Long Island.

There were two workout rooms: a large room for men and much smaller room for women. The also had a jacuzzi and a pool.

Within a few years, some clubs began to provide trainers. The best clubs employed qualified trainers with the best equipment and a clean environment.

At seventy-one years of age, I joined De-Fine Fitness in Roslyn the week it opened, and have trained three times a week for the past twenty years.

Craig Hatchett owns De-Fine Fitness and has been my personal trainer the entire time. Now in my ninetiess, Craig has kept me strong and healthy far longer than I would otherwise have been!

In 1959, Castro was declared the new premier of Cuba. Alaska became the fifty-first state. Buddy Holly died in a plane crash.

CHAPTER 14
The Rest of (Our) Lives; Becoming an Innovative Entrepreneur

In Brooklyn, New York, I was honorably discharged from the army. Pat picked me up and we drove to her parents' house on 7 Linden Boulevard in Great Neck. We stayed there for almost eight weeks before we found our own apartment.

In 1960, Great Neck was where upwardly mobile families wanted to live. It is comprised of multiple towns, such as Kensington, Great Neck Estates, Kings Point, Sands Point, Russell Gardens, University Gardens, and others.

The center of activity was the temple you belonged to (reformed, conservative, or orthodox) and/or which country club you were a member of (Glen Oaks, Fresh Meadows, or Lake Success).

Everyone patronized the kosher deli, the two movie theaters, and stores of all kinds. The commercial center of town was Middle Neck Road.

Living with my in-laws was very comfortable and the food was the best, but we needed to find our own apartment. We found what we were looking for at 20 Clent Road. It was within walking distance of Middle Neck Road.

At $150 per month, our two-bedroom apartment featured a small terrace and garage space for one car.

While Pat and her mother shopped for furniture, I resumed work at Fuller Tool Company. During my two-year stint in the army, the factory had moved from the Bronx at Garrison and Faille Streets to a far larger space on Webster Avenue. The daily trip from Great Neck, over the Whitestone Bridge to the east Bronx, took about thirty-five minutes. The bridge toll was still twenty-five cents each way. Gas cost thirty-five cents per gallon, and the New York City subway, busses, and the Staten Island Ferry were just a nickel each way.

My job at Fuller Tool Company was as a salesman, except that I was now responsible for far more territory than before I left for the army. Air travel had become easier, and more cities were accessible by air. Hotels were still the best place to stay as the motel industry was in its infancy.

Under President Eisenhower, the country was building a nationwide system of high-speed interstate highways. Still, at the time, most roads went through small towns, each of which had its own police department and judges.

On one occasion, I was late for an appointment to see a customer in Greenville, North Carolina. As I was driving along a rural, single-lane road, I came upon a funeral procession. They were moving at about twenty-five miles per hour. Not wanting to be late, I went around the procession until I reached the hearse at the front of the line. Two motorcycle cops were escorting the lead vehicle and one of them waved me over to the side of the road.

My New York state license plates gave me away as a "Yankee." The officer informed me it was the law in North Carolina that you cannot pass a funeral. He ordered me to follow him to the local judge.

When we arrived at the courthouse, the clerk informed me that the judge had gone fishing. I could wait for him in the county jail and he would hear my case the next day, or I could pay a fifty-dollar fine and be on my way. Naturally, I paid up, but that left me very short of cash.

The old roadways that linked local towns through the country were lucrative speed traps for travelers passing through. The posted speed limit could drop from fifty miles per hour to fifteen miles per hour without warning and a cop would pull you over. Either you paid the cash fine (checks not accepted) or spent the night in jail. The interstate highway system would eventually eliminate this form of extortion.

On May 25, 1960, David Fuller was born at Long Island Jewish Hospital. In 1960, Dwight Eisenhower was president. John F. Kennedy announced his run for president against Richard Nixon. Adolph Eichmann was captured in Argentina. The Beatles had their first public performance.

We brought David home to our new apartment on Clent Road and hired a baby nurse, Miss Jeager, to help. She was a wonderful baby nurse and helped Pat make a quick recovery. David was an easy baby, which was fortunate for Pat as I was traveling for Fuller Tool Company a good deal of the time. I must admit, however, that when I was home, 99 percent of the baby's care fell to Pat.

One day, while I was babysitting, David needed a diaper change badly, and I didn't quite know how to handle the situation. I decided it was a good time to visit our friend Carole Aronson a few minutes away in Great Neck. Problem solved.

David grew into a good looking and talented young man. He loves playing the guitar and has a tribute band that plays Grateful Dead music. As a kid, David made friends easily and friends he made back then are still among his best friends today.

After attending Miami University School of Music, he joined me in business, but it wasn't in the cards. He has been a senior underwriter for the New York state mortgage authority.

David Fuller married Rachel Weiner, our beautiful and talented daughter-in-law. Our grandchild Max is the joy of our life.

The years 1959 and 1960 were very good for Pat and me. We had a nice apartment, a new baby, and many good friends. I played golf on weekends at Bethpage (public) Golf Course with my brother-in-law Jerry Hahn. We hired a "runner" for five dollars to sign us up at 5:00 a.m. so we could secure an 8:30 tee time.

Pat and I made our first trip to Florida in 1961. With our friends Roberta and Kenny Lonoff, we stayed at my parents' small apartment in Miami while they were away. We stayed out too late, played some golf, went fishing, drank too much, and danced until dawn. We had a great time!

Frank Sinatra was at the height of his fame, having recently starred in *From Here to Eternity* with Deborah Kerr. Frank was appearing at the Fontainebleau Hotel. We all wanted to go. The cover charge was fifteen dollars per person, and you were obliged to order dinner before the show started. This was going to be an expensive night, but we were excited to see Sinatra in person.

By the time he came out on stage, it was already 11:00 p.m. and most of the audience had already had too much to drink. A heckler in the audience shouted some remarks at Frank.

With that, Sinatra shouted back at the heckler, "I don't need this." He disappeared from the stage. The theater fell silent. Someone came out front and announced that Mr. Sinatra would not be performing that evening. We were asked to leave the theater. There would be no refunds.

After that debacle, Pat refused to listen to Frank Sinatra sing or watch any of his movies.

Chapter 15
The Bronx

The US and the world economy was expanding rapidly. People were buying homes, new interstate highways were being built, and airlines were extending their routes. There was no shooting war that involved the United States. However, the Cold War between the United States and the Soviet Union was growing hotter, and Castro was getting cozy with the Russians.

Business was good. American factories made the best products in the world, and hand tools were no exception. The factory was in the Bronx at Garrison and Faile streets in a former Buick sales and service facility.

We used the bottom floor for packaging and shipping and the top floor for storage. The floors were connected by a conveyor belt that had been installed where a staircase had been.

One day, a builiding inspector arrived without warning. After a cursory examination of the building, he issued a summons that stated the conveyor belt was a safety violation of the New York City building code. We had thirty days to remove the conveyor belt and restore the staircase to its original specifications.

If we failed to do so, the company would be fined $1000 per day until we were following the building code.

My father called me into his office and closed the door.

"This is what you are going to do." He handed me an envelope which contained five $100 bills and the name and address of the building inspector.

"Be at his office at exactly 2:00 p.m. tomorrow and give him the envelope. In exchange, he will give you the original violation document stamped 'Void.' Say nothing and immediately return to the office. Nothing will go wrong if you follow my instructions."

He was right: nothing went wrong, and we never replaced the stairs or removed the converyor belt.

What I took away from this event was that my father had put me at risk of a criminal felony, attempted bribery of a government official. If convicted, the penalty would be five years in prison.

Industrial Plastics Inc. in Caldwell, New Jersey had been providing Fuller Tool Company with extruded plastic screwdriver handles and assembling the finished product for five years. Bernie Fuller decided to buy the company to insure a reliable and steady supply and to reduce the cost of their most important product: unbreakable plastic handle screwdrivers.

The owner of Industrial Plastics retired but the factory manager and all the workers kept their jobs. At least once every week for the next few years, I would drive out to Caldwell, New Jersey to revise the production schedule, payroll, inventory, and other basic functions. Everything was usually in order. The decision to buy the company had increased the profit margins on our most important product line: screwdrivers

At the end of World War 2, Bernie Fuller began a series of buying trips to Europe. The first was to Sweden. In those post-war years, he would fly to London from Idlewild Airport (renamed John F. Kennedy International Airport after Kennedy was assassinated in 1963) on a new Boeing four-engine plane called *Constellation* to Gander Newfoundland for refueling. Then, he had another six-hour flight to London and a short flight to Oslo.

In a small city in the north of Sweden, Bernie found a factory that manufactured high-quality chisels. We imported the chisel (blades only) to New Jersey where our new "unbreakable" plastic handles were applied. Before this innovation, carpenters' chisels had wooden handles that would split if hammered too hard or too long. The new, extruded plastic handle would never break or split. In addition, the new plastic handles cost less than wood handles. Fuller's unbreakable plastic handle chisels were an instant success.

In the 1950s, Europe was the prime source of Fuller Tools except for screwdrivers. Pliers and carbide steel masonry drills came from England, files from Portugal, and chisels from Sweden. Under President Eisenhower, both the US economy and Fuller Tool Co. were rapidly expanding.

Chapter 16
Pine Hollow CC

At about this time, I became a member of Pine Hollow Country Club. Pine Hollow was not my first choice, and therein lies a story.

As I wrote earlier, my father-in-law Jerry Green had been a member of Glen Oaks Club since 1925. Jerry's uncle Harry had been a founder of the club some years earlier. The Green family hoped that Pat and I would join Glen Oaks when we were financially able to do so.

There would be no problem joining as both of our families had been members of Glen Oaks for many years. I would be interviewed by the membership committee but if no member objected, I would be granted full membership. As the son of a member under forty years of age, the initiation fee of $20,000 would be waived.

However, if a regular member objected to my membership (known as a "blackball"), my membership could not proceed.

Therefore, it came as a shock that a certain club member had blackballed my application. As a result, I was denied membership to Glen Oaks Country Club.

Being blackballed by a member of a respected Country Club can be problematic. It says to everyone that there may be something wrong with your character, your ethics, or your background.

This was very upsetting to me, to Pat, and to Pat's family.

However, it did not bother my father as he was the member who had prevented me from joining Glen Oaks.

When I found out, I confronted him with this disturbing revelation. He did not deny it. When pressed for an explanation, he replied, "There are plenty of other golf courses on Long Island that you could join. I prefer that you do not belong to the same club as me. I do not want to be known as Buzz Fuller's father. Glen Oaks is my club. Join your own golf club."

Some might call it tough love, but I believe it was something quite different. The reader can draw his or her own conclusion.

In happier times

Chapter 17
Discharged

After two years' service with the US army, I returned to the family business. Screwdrivers were still 90 percent of all sales. Only 10 percent of Fuller Tool products were imported. Over the coming years, the ratio would be reversed.

Most of my time was dedicated to calling on customers from Maine to New Orleans and west to California. We did not use commission sales agents, so the entire country was covered by me, Jim Rienthal, and our Vice President of Sales, Johnny Weil.

Sears Roebuck had long been the largest retailer in the world. My father called on Sears in Chicago for many years before he eventually succeeded in selling them Fuller screwdrivers. It was just the beginning of a long and mutually profitable relationship.

At its peak, Fuller Tools were stocked by 400 hardware distributors and displayed in every neighhood hardware store.

True Value Hardware Co-op was the brainchild of John Cotter. Based on the model of farm co-ops, a hardware retail store could purchase merchandise at lower prices and enjoy the benefit of national advertising. At year's end, the member store earned a rebate based on their annual purchases. It was a winning formula.

In 1940, however, True Value was struggling to survive. Traditional hardware distributors told their vendors they had to choose between selling to them or the co-ops.

Bernie Fuller and John Cotter had both struggled to be taken seriously. Ignoring the threats, Fuller Tool Company was one of the few sources willing to do business with John Cotter.

By the 60s hardware co-ops dominated the retail hardware industry. True Value Co-op had a membership of more than 6000 hardware stores, and two other co-ops controlled another 10,000 retail stores. The old-line hardware distributors that had controlled the hardware industry were rapidly disappearing.

It was during this period that I met Danny Cotter. Dan was my age and the son of John Cotter. The friendship between my father and Danny's father would continue between Danny and me.

Between 1960 and 1967, I learned the vital role of packaging and display. Most hand tools, especially low-cost screwdrivers, are a "commodity." When there is little difference between your brand and the competition, the most attractive and informative package will always sell better.

From the time Fuller Tool began in 1935, Frank Fox Printing Company, located at Broadway at 23rd Street, provided all the printing and packaging needs of the company. Bernie Fuller relied on Frank to prepare the artwork, write sales copy, print catalog pages, design and produce packaging for every Fuller Tool product. That is, until I met Miles Godin and his partner Burt Hersch. At the time, the partners had just started an advertising agency called Burton-Miles Advertising.

Pat and I met Miles and his new wife Judy at an engagement party for a mutual friend in Great Neck. We were all in our mid-twenties. When Miles told me what he did, I invited him to meet me at our office to discuss a new project that had not yet been given to Frank Fox. I wanted a fresh look and maybe Miles could provide it. To avoid controversy, I personally assured Frank that his firm would continue to be our primary source of printing.

Mile's ideas were new and exciting. Together, we created new package designs, in full color, with illustrations and sales "copy." We would collaborate after business hours at each other's homes. Our objective was to upgrade the appearance of Fuller Tools to achieve greater market penetration. We succeeded beyond all expectations. As sales grew, so did my confidence in my ability to expand the business my father had started.

I began to work directly with our sources in the United States and eventually in both Europe and Japan.

Chapter 18
Japan with Jerry Hahn

My first trip to Japan was with Jerry Hahn and it was memorable. Jerry had started buying steak knife blades from a factory in the same city where we both had sources.

Traveling in Japan with Jerry Hahn was a novel experience. At six feet four inches, he was constantly ducking below the low ceilings.

June Uchida had planned for us to stay at a Japanese *rikoban* (hotel) in Sanjo city about one hundred miles from Hiroshima. In this small city, high-quality factories were producing hand tools including pliers, hammers, and wrenches. Others made high-quality carving knives and various kitchen tools.

The rikoban had been alerted of our arrival and had prepared the hotel bath for us. The bath was like a very large Jacuzzi but without water jets. It had taken all day to bring the bath to the proper temperature.

The bath was located off the main lobby and had a clear glass door. Jerry and I entered the room fully clothed and proceed to undress. We noticed some water valves, soap, washcloths, and two small stools to sit on. Clearly, the soap was there to use in the bath. We climbed into the very hot water and began to soap ourselves until clean, and then relaxed and enjoyed the warm water.

Upon getting out of the bath, we struggled to dry ourselves with the very small towel provided. There were also two robes laid out. Unfortunately, the small robe was not intended for someone as tall as Jerry. You can imagine the result.

Walking quickly across the lobby, we passed the other hotel guests and hurried to our small room.

After several minutes, we heard loud shouting and suddenly a very angry man burst into our room followed closely by June Uchida. It was the hotel manager. Shouting in Japanese, he pointed an accusatory finger at us. After a while, he stormed out of our room. What was that all about?

As we learned later, in Japan, the bath itself is used to relax in after you have washed and cleaned yourself with soap and water from spigots in the wall while trying to stay seated on a tiny wooden stool.

Only after you are clean do you enter the bath. We did not know the process and, in our ignorance, had immersed our soapy bodies into the clean bath water.

As a result, the bath had to be drained, scrubbed clean, refilled, and heated again before it could be used by other guests. It was not an auspicious start in this strange but wonderful country.

June Uchida was our company buying agent and translator. A few years before this event, my father had lured June away from the trading company he had retained to source new factories for us in Japan. June was assigned to manage our account. Her English was quite good. She was single and smart.

Most trading companies at that time were "double dipping," i.e. taking a sales commission from the factory while at the same time charging their American clients a buying commission. Another serious concern was when a factory agreed to a lower price, they would try to make it up by lowering the quality of the product. Not understanding the language made it risky. You would not know if you had made a good deal until the shipping container arrived at your loading dock, and sometimes not until your customers called to complain

With the buying agent on your payroll, you could avoid double dipping and be assured your quality standards were met before your letter of credit could be paid to the factory. This was my first opportunity to learn the machines and methods required to produce good quality pliers, hammers, adjustable wrenches, and other basic hand tools in the rapidly expanding line of Fuller Tools.

It was important to establish good relationships with the various factory owners. In Japan, certain formalities are observed before you bring up business matters. Primary among them was to have a cup of green tea and smoke a Japanese cigarette. These were nothing like Marlboro (my brand at the time) but were hand rolled and very strong. The tea was not red like Lipton, but a watery green color and without sugar.

To make matters worse, if the meeting was held in winter, the office would be freezing cold. On the other hand, as your host, a Japanese factory owner would ask about your wife and children and your favorite sport. The atmosphere quickly warmed, and after a while, the tea didn't taste so bad.

The factories at that time, around 1963, were not as automated as they would later become. Forging, grinding, and polishing was all labor intensive. Dozens of men sat on low stools at grinders. Overhead, large, belt-driven wheels provided power to the machines. The men would not look up but continue grinding or polishing on a specific part of a wrench, plier, or hammer.

The typical workday was ten hours each day, six days a week. Wages were about 10 percent that of an American worker doing the same job in an air-conditioned union factory. The air was filled with metal dust, and the only light came through dirty glass windows. Every tool was eventually transformed from a dull steel grey into a shiny, bright, chrome-plated, fully functional tool bearing the brand name Fuller.

During the period between 1963 to 1967, I made buying trips to Japan, Italy, Portugal, and England. Fuller Tool Co. was growing at a fast clip and every month exceeded the prior month.

It became apparent that we had outgrown the bulding in the Bronx. Since most of the key executives lived on Long Island, it made sense to find a location nearer to where they lived.

My father gave me the job of finding a suitable location in Queens. I had no knowledge of the real estate business. The first thing I did was to use the Queens Yellow Pages to find a commercial real estate broker. Fortunately, the first broker I called was extremely knowlegable and had many listings in Queens. In two weeks, I looked at no less than twelve potential buildings. There were some good opportunities in Long Island City, but traffic in the area was always heavy and the neighborhood was unsafe.

We needed at least 50,000 square feet, with high ceilings, and loading bays. Eventually, I was shown a property in Whitestone, Queens, on 10th Avenue close to the Whitestone Bridge. There were two buildings and plenty of parking space for employees. Since there were now two companies (Fuller Tool and Regent Sheffield Ltd.), it had potential. I took my father and Jerry Hahn to see it and they both agreed that it would become the new location for Fuller Tool and Regent Sheffield.

Fuller Realty Corporation was created to purchase both buildings and to collect rent from both Fuller Tool and Regent Sheffield. Bernie Fuller was the sole owner of Fuller Realty Corp.

I was assigned the job of moving the entire company from the Bronx to Queens on a tight timeline. New offices were built, worktables purchased, storage racks installed, and new lighting fixtures and ceiling fans installed. We repladed the windows, installed air conditioning, and new bathrooms. Transporting the inventory and equipment took two full days, but it all went off as planned.

Chapter 19
Steve Gutman

I met Steve Gutman in 1951 when he was seventeen years old. Steve was my roommate at Lehigh University. After seventy years, we remain close friends.

After graduating from college and earning a master's degree in finance from New York University, Steve married Carol Fredricks.

Steve's career included several years on Wall Street and twenty years as president of the New York Jets football team, then owned by Leon Hess (Hess Oil).

When Leon Hess passed away, Steve negotiated the sale of the Jets team to Woody Johnson of Johnson and Johnson Inc. On completion of the sale, Steve was generously compensated and soon thereafter retired.

My sister Dee, Jerry Hahn, and their three boys Jonathon, Ricki, and Steven lived in a three-bedroom house in Roslyn, New York. The family needed a larger house.

Jerry soon found something he felt would be suitable. The house was off Glen Cove Road at Simonson Road in Greenville, Long Island. It had been built seventy-five years earlier by the Vanderbilts during the Gilded Age.

The main house had fifteen rooms, seven bedrooms, plus separate servants' quarters. The living room fireplace was so large, five or six adults could stand inside of it.

The estate featured formal gardens, woods, and streams on twelve highly cultivated acres. Jerry purchased a farm tractor to mow his beautiful Kentucky bluegrass.

Jerry furnished it with heavy, very dark, antique furniture he had shipped from England. Dee and Jerry named their new home Masada after the renowned mountain-top fortress in Israel.

Helen Fuller was apoplectic. She said Jerry Hahn had overreached ("Who does he think he is?") and told everyone that Jerry was a fool. She could not accept the fact that the decision to buy the house and property was made without consulting her and her husband. After all, Jerry had "nothing" when he married their daughter.

Helen Fuller never stepped foot on the property. In addition, she made it clear that Jerry was no longer admired or trusted.

Eventually, Masada became a source of friction that would lead to the end of my sister's marriage after twenty-five years. Dee filed for divorce. Soon after the divorce, Jerry sold Masada for a nice profit.

For once, Helen was right. The big house on Simonson Road in Old Brookville, Long Island, had been a mistake.

Chapter 20
Settllling Down

I realized that accounting was a vital area of business about which I had only rudimentary knowledge, even with a degree in business administration.

Ed Rienthal had been with the company for many years. Although not an accountant, Ed oversaw product cost accounting and purchasing. Since each product had to be priced profitably, Ed had developed various formulas to account for every element of product cost, from the Japanese factory floor to our factory door, to the cost of cash discounts, commissions, ad allowances, and other factors.

Ed worked with me for many hours until he felt he had no more to teach me. In my future business endeavors, these lessons would soon prove invaluable.

In the spring of 1964, Pat was pregnant. It was a difficult pregnancy, and Pat was in the hospital for two months before Susan was born on July 26, 1964.

Having successfully negotiated a commercial real estate purchase, Pat sent me out to find a suitable house for our family. I promptly retained a broker and visited several dozen homes, often with one-year-old David in tow.

One day, I visited a house on Sugar Maple Drive in Roslyn. It was a four-bedroom split level on one-quarter of an acre, built only nine months before.

The master bathroom was wallpapered with blue butterflies. I called Pat and described the blue butterflies. The house was owned by a couple in the midst of a divorce. They needed to sell, and we loved the house.

The deal was done for less than $30,000, including fixtures and brand-new appliances. My older sister Dorothy observed that our new house was a nice "starter" house, for now.

Susan was a very different child than her brother David. From the day she was born, she was "vocal." Before she could talk, she would scream, and well after she could talk, she was still screaming. At the same time, Susan was a good student. Her grades were above average. She was also very athletic. At an early age, we started her on golf lessons, swimming lessons, and judo.

Susan breezed through high school and graduated from Brandeis University. After graduating from Cardozo Law School, Susan passed the New York bar exam. Her first legal job was with the law office of New York City. Rudy Giuliani was the mayor. Today, Susan has her own law firm in Seattle, where she lives with her spouse Julie. Her youthful "screaming" has been replace by thoughtful, intelligent conversation.

While still living at 20 Clent Road in Great Neck, we made friends with other young couples. Bob Johnson was a newly married man in our building. He worked as a "detail man" for a drug company. The job required calling on physicians to convince them to prescribe whatever drugs his pharmaceutical company was currently promoting. I found Bob to have a very orderly mind and he was a hard worker.

On a hunch, I offered him a job as my assistant at Fuller Tool. The choice was a good one, as Bob quickly became a team player. About a year later, Ed Rienthal suddenly died. Ed had been my father's administrative assistant.

Bob Johnson took over for Ed. From then on, Bob Johnson became my father's confidant and "right hand man." Within two years, Bernie Fuller gave Bob a cash bonus so that Bob could buy a house in Westbury, Long Island. In time, Bob Johnson's loyalty to my father, rather than to me, would prove instrumental in preserving his job. I could not blame him, but it still hurt.

My office in the new Whitestone factory was directly next to my father's office. We spoke constantly, and I always sought his advice. As time went on, he gave me more and more responsibility. I was involved in almost every aspect of the business. There were, however, two areas that remained out of bounds.

The first was his close relationship with our largest customer, Sears Roebuck. Several times per year, my father would travel to Chicago and spend three days with Mr. Charlie Dunlap, vice president in charge of hand tools. Fuller Tool Company had become the largest supplier of screwdrivers to Sears Roebuck and Company.

Sears Roebuck was Bernie Fuller's personal account. At Sears headquarters in Chicago, many issues were always under review, including pricing, sales, quality control, new items, advertising, and promotions.

The other subject never discussed was his frequent visits to our sources in Japan accompanied by June Uchida. Ms. Uchida was responsible for finding and supervising our factory sources in Japan. One time, he brought back a souvenir from a famous resort. There were rumors.

It had been a mere eighteen years since the end of World War 2. Japan was still recovering from the destruction of its manufacturing facilities. American quality standards were still superior. There was a lot of work to do.

Our Japanese imports grew rapidly. Fuller Tool Company set up a new company, Fuller Orient. June Uchida was made president of Fuller Orient. Her salary and expenses were paid by Fuller Orient and included an apartment/office in Osaka that Bernie used while in Japan

It was an open secret to everyone at Fuller Tool that my father and Ms. Uchida had more in common than hand tools.

Bernie would hide his correspondence with Ms. Uchida under the blotter on his desk. He also had a post office box at the Little Neck Post Office. When June Uchida came to New York, she stayed with my folks at their apartment in Great Neck.

While the "affair" wasn't open, I am sure my mother was aware of it. However, she let it go if he was discreet (sort of). In exchange, Helen made the important decisions for the family while he ran the business.

September 11, 2001

Islamist extremists from Saudi Arabia hijacked four commercial jet airplanes. Two jets crashed directly into the twin towers of the World Trade Center in New York City. Both towers collapsed and more than three thousand people were killed.

A third passenger aircraft deliberately slammed into the Pentagon, the top military building in Washington, DC.

A fourth plane was aiming for the White House, but the passengers brought it down in a field in rural Pennsylvania. There were no survivors.

When the World Trade Center towers fell, I watched it happen while working out with my trainer at a local gym.

It was hard for anyone to make sense of what was happening when the first tower simply collapsed. Within minutes, the second tower fell.

Like most people who lived in the New York metropolitan area, we either knew someone who worked there or who died there. One of these people was the brother of my trainer, Craig Hatchett.

As we watched both towers fall, Craig whispered to me that his brother's company was located on a high floor of the south tower.

Several hours later, Craig's mother called to say that his brother did not go to work that day. He was safe.

Craig has been my personal trainer for more than twenty years, ever since that day in September 2001.

Chapter 21
The 60's

On November 23, 1963, John F. Kennedy was assassinated.

You always remember exactly where you were when big events happened. On that day, I was in our new offices in Whitestone. Suddenly, our factory foreman burst into the office and shouted the news that President John F. Kennedy had been shot in Dallas, Texas and was in critical condition.

Later that day, President Kennedy died of massive wounds to his head.

That same day, on the flight back to Washington, DC, Mrs. Kennedy, in her bloodstained dress, stood behind Lyndon Johnson as he was sworn in as the new president.

That night, our family attended temple services. The rabbi delivered an amazing sermon. It would take many months for most people, especially younger people, to get back to normal.

Eventually, my father began to lose interest in the everyday demands of running what had become a large company. We had about seventy-five workers in the factory and perhaps fifteen in the office. His frequent trips to Japan and Chicago were tiring.

Sears had changed from the old days. The buyers were younger and didn't care about the history of Fuller Tool and Sears. It was all before their time. By 1963,

Bernie had been building the company from the Depression era, through World War 2, and into the rapid recovery in post-war America.

He wanted to spend more time at his condo in Miami, but he needed someone to run the everyday business.

In 1964, over the objections of my mother, Bernie made me president of Fuller Tool Company and himself chairman of the board.

They had a small apartment in Miami, near the nursing home where Grandma Anna Manchyk lived. They now could spend most of each winter in Florida. They played golf during the day and bridge with friends in the evening. Everything was running smoothly back home.

My sister June Sloan, our bookkeeper Lillian, and Bob Johnson reported directly to my father in Florida. Steve Gutman, Ronald Mandler, and the plant manager reported to me, as did the office staff. Office politics were prevalent, buy I stayed out of it.

Chapter 22
My First Startup (with Training Wheels)

During the decade of the 60s, retailing (at least in the United States) was changing fast. Discount stores were taking business away from retail giants like Sears Roebuck. These new outlets carried everything from clothes to hardware and automotive products. By cutting out the middleman (wholesalers), they could sell everything at a discount.

By purchasing directly from the manufacturer, they sold everything at 40 percent less than Sears or Macy's. The public loved them. Spartan Stores, Zayre, Two Guys, Woolco, and EJ Korvette began to appear on the retail scene. To me, they were the future of hardware retailing.

The introduction of discount stores threatened the existence of smaller neighborhood hardware stores, which at the time were the base of Fuller Tool Company sales.

However, I believed we could not ignore the rise of discount stores. I devised a marketing plan that would not antagonize our base of hardware distributors and thousands of local hardware retailers.

Bernie Fuller had no interest in selling to discount stores, believing they would undercut the prices of neighborhood hardware stores. I shared his concern but offered a solution. Fuller Tool could fully support the hardware distributors and the new discount stores at the same time.

The concept I presented to Fuller Tool Company was to create a totally separate company with a new name, new staff, and a different location.

The new company would be dedicated exclusively to marketing hand tools to discount stores. The presentation, packaging, and marketing of the line would be unlike our Fuller Brand of tools or of any other brand. Although the new line would look different, the products would be produced by Fuller Tool. It was a win-win situation.

Every package of pliers, screwdrivers, wrenches, hammers, and other items would be uniform in appearance except for specific illustrations and copy. All products, when displayed together, would make a powerful display that demanded a shopper's attention.

The consumer could easily find any size and type of hand tool in a single location without a sales clerk. In a small hardware store, all pliers are displalyed together, all saws together, and so on.

The new company would break with tradition by requiring the full line be displayed together and not separated by item category.

Creating a new brand of hand tools exclusively for large discount stores was my idea, and my father told me that if it failed, it would be on me, and he would have nothing to do with it.

I named my new company Award Tools Inc. Fuller Tool Company would produce tools branded Award and paid for under letters of credit. All other requirements for the operation of the business would be sourced locally and purchased by Award.

Although I had to sign a personal guarantee, Chase Manhattan Bank approved a loan to get us started. I immediately made two hires: Jim Braddock to locate and set up the new facility and a sales manager, Marty Rieger, who had previously been a salesman for Fuller Tool Co.

It is impossible to measure the time, energy, and luck you need to create, build, and successfully market a totally new product line.

3M Company used Award packaging in a national advertisement.

What does it take to establish a new business?

"Find a Need, and Package It!"

- Have a well-developed "vision" of your new company.
- Know your product line.
- Secure your finances.
- Know where, or how, to find suppliers.
- Negotiate each component cost and establish pricing.
- Design effective packaging and sales copy.
- Set up a sales and marketing program.
- Identify and visit your most important prospects
- Mangage every crisis!

It was 1965. Award Tool Co. was my first solo venture in creating a totally new enterprise.

Award depended on Fuller Tool to supply our basic product line. Everthing else, including rent for a warehouse, new steel storage racks, worktables, packaging machines, store displays, and so on we paid for from our intial bank loan.

It took five months for Fuller Tool to produce and deliver the full line of of Award hand tools and another month to package the line for delivery. All we needed were customers!

The first chain of discount stores to purchase Award Tools was E.J. Korvette, the undisputed leader among all discount stores at the time. With Korvette on board, most of the other big discount stores followed. Before the end of our first year, Award sales exceeded one million dollars (about three million dollars today).

Hardware distributors never knew that Award Tools were produced by Fuller Tool Company.

We had achieved the goal of increasing the total sales of Fuller Tool Company without upsetting 400 hardware distributors and 25,000 mom and pop hardware stores.

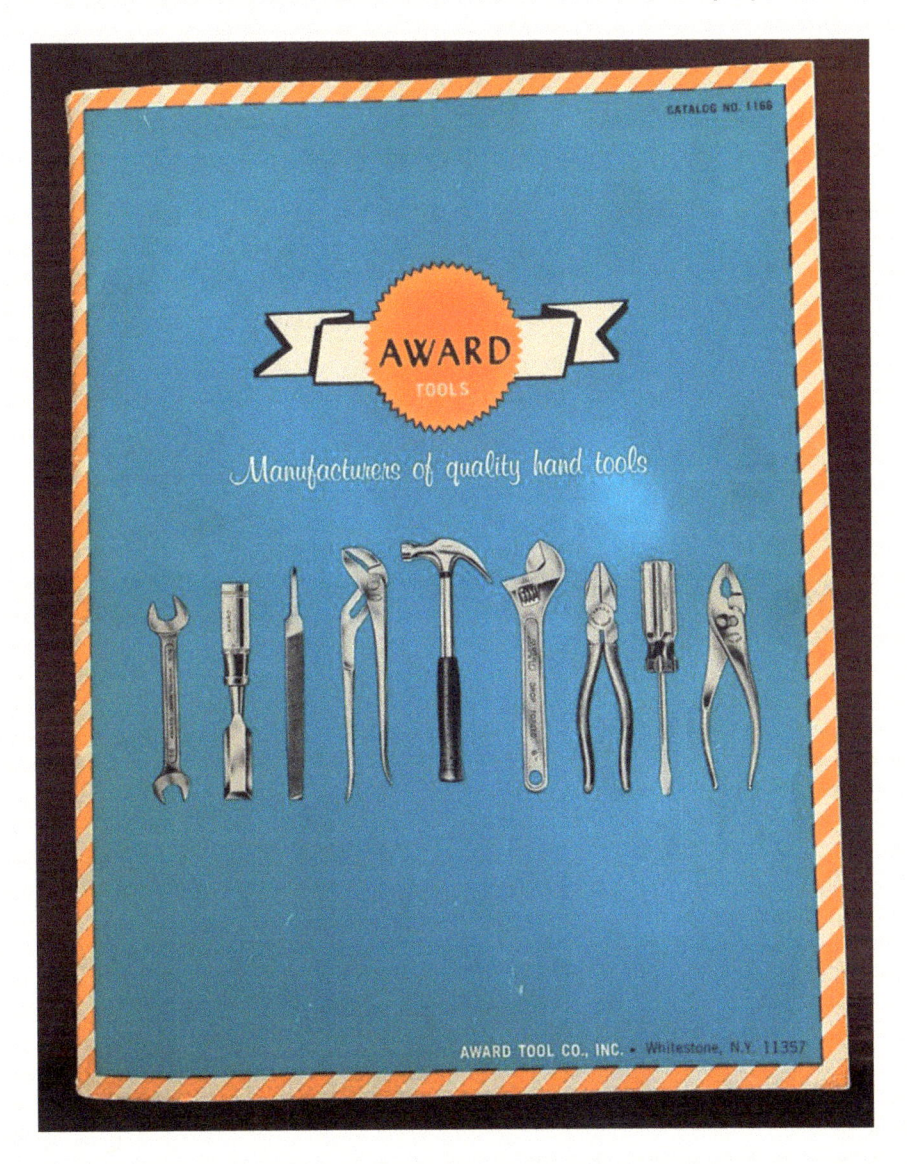

The first year of Award required a lot of time as I was also President of Fuller Tool Company.

By 1965, my father was fifty-eight years of age and spending six months of the year in Florida, traveling with my mother, and spending at least two weeks in Japan. They enjoyed ocean cruises and golf at Glen Oaks Country Club. The day-to-day management of Fuller Tool Company and Award was left to me.

With the support of a terrific team at Fuller Tool and a booming economy, the company was growing steadily. Steve Gutman joined the company and improved the efficiency and quality of the products made by Industrial Plastics, our new factory in Caldwell, New Jersey.

I hired a close college friend, Ronald Mandler, for special accounts. The first thing he wanted us to do was purchase a new IBM computer system. The new computer was expensive but revealed valuable information regarding customer sales, the items they purchased, monthly and annual volume, items carried, customer reorders, payment records, and other vital sales information. It was the start of the Information Age.

Chapter 23
Fun Time

Pat and I decided to go on a cruise to the Caribbean. I made reservations on the SS *France* for a ten-day voyage departing from New York in two weeks.

We invited twenty of our friends to a bon-voyage party in our stateroom. It was wonderful.

During the entire trip, the seas were calm and the weather was perfect. Everything was perfect, especially the French food and service. The ship stopped at the most popular islands. We bought souvenirs and gifts for everyone, and literally danced the nights away. It was the "caviar of cruises" with plenty of caviar every day.

At home, life was going along well. David was six years old, Susan was two. We had a mother's helper living with us. Every Wedndeday, Maurice would thoroughly clean the house.

The war in Vietnam was making headlines, along with vivid TV coverage. Lyndon Johnson was president, having succeeded to that office after Kennedy was assassinated in 1963. Lyndon Johnson was elected on his own two years later.

As a young member of Pine Hollow Country Club, I played golf on Saturday and Sunday mornings. On weekend afternoons in the summer, the whole family enjoyed the pool at the club.

We found new friends in our community. Ruth and Maurice Felber visited us from London. We attended their son David's Bar Mitzvah, across the pond in London.

Chapter 24
All is Well (until it wasn't)

January 1967

US President Ronald Reagan was sworn in as the thirty-third governor of California. The crew of Gus Grissom, Ed White, and Roger Chaffee were killed in a fire in the Apollo Command Module during a preflight test at Cape Canaveral. Color television became widely available.

A Visitor from India

Ashok Birla was the scion of one of the wealthiest industrial/political families in India and had earned a masters degree at Birla University.

Ashok wanted us to buy twist drills from one of their many factories in India. We did not have twist drills in our line at the time and the samples he showed us ere quite good. The cost was extremely low.

We would provide samples of top-quality US-made twist drills as examples of what we required. If they could produce the same quality, I would go to Bombay to inspect the factory and place a trial purchase order. Ashok assured me they could produce the quality required.

In due course, the samples arrived and were sent to a testing lab. They samples were excellent. My trip to Bombay was confirmed.

In May 1967, Muhammad Ali was indicted for refusal to serve in the US army.

We had become close friends with neighbors Ed and Lorraine Feldman. Ed was working for 7 Arts Productions, a large entertainment company, which was producing a new Broadway musical based on the life of Sophie Tucker. The lead role was to be played by an unknown singer from Brooklyn, New York.

Ed asked me over to listen to a demo recording of a song from the show. He wanted me to hear it because he was convinced the new girl was going to be star. I had a good ear for music and told him I would give him my honest opinion.

It was a good song with catchy lyrics. The singer wasn't bad, but I advised Ed not to get too excited. Being charitable, I said she had a good voice, but it was nothing special.

The song was "Lovers," sung by Barbra Streisand. Within a few months, the show was a big hit, and Barbra was the toast of Broadway. I sure was wrong about Barbra!

Ed Feldman, a kid from the Bronx, went on to become a successful movie producer in Hollywood. Over his long career, Ed produced many noteworthy films including *Witness*, *The Truman Show*, *101 Dalmatians*, *Green Card*, and *Save the Tiger,* to name just a few.

Cannes via Bombay India

It was April 1967. I was preparing for my trip to India to visit Ashok Birla's twist drill factory in Bombay. Lorraine Feldman asked Pat if she would like to join them at the Cannes Film Festival in early May. We could celebrate Pat's thirty-third birthday in Cannes.

It sounded like fun! I would fly to Bombay and complete my work in four days. From Bombay, I would fly to Cairo, then onto Rome, and finally to the Italian Riviera. Meanwhile, Pat would fly over and meet the Feldmans in Cannes. We would attend the world premiere of a new movie for 7 Arts called *You're a Big Boy Now* directed by a total unknown named Francis Ford Coppola.

Business before Pleasure

I landed in Bombay around midnight. The temperature was still in the nineties with humidity to match. My first impression of India was not a good one. The streets were filled with desperately poor people, outdoor stalls, motorbikes. pushcarts, kids begging, and cows in the street! The air was filled with smoke and smelled bad.

Outside of the city center, large families lived on bare ground or at best in tents. There were few cars and many bicycles. A "cab" was a thin man pulling a rickshaw-like contraption for five cents a ride.

Above all was the smell of food cooking, along with garbage and human waste. It had been like this for centuries with few signs of improvement.

Ashok Birla had put me up in five-star hotel. There were servants at every turn: one to unpack and put away my clothes, another to polish shoes, and a still another to provide ice, newspapers, and anything I might need.

I could not process the vast difference between America and India.

The Birla family was well known and respected throughout India. Birla factories employed thousands. Birla University graduates occupied high business and government positions. They were super rich.

Ashok invited me to his "palace" to meet some of his friends. Uniformed soldiers with weapons stood at attention as our Rolls Royce approached the huge iron gates. Inside, the walls were lined with photos of Birla family members posing with world leaders including Gandhi, Eisenhower, John Kennedy, and the prime minister of Austria Konrad Adenauer.

During the three days that followed, Ashok and I concluded our deal for twist drills, which he agreed would conform to US specifications and would be branded by Fuller Tool Company.

After business was concluded each day, we dined at his club. We later toured several drinking clubs, although consuming alcohol was banned to the public.

One afternoon, Ashok invited me to play a round of golf with him at the Bombay Country Club (originally built by the English occupiers). I said I would like to but had no clubs or shoes. In short order, a brand-new set of golf clubs and shoes appeared.

Playing golf in India is much different from playing golf in the United States. Each player is assigned a (barefoot) caddie. Ashok prevailed upon the club pro and his assistant to join us for nine holes. At about 150 yards down the fairway was another group of four small boys who did not move away when we teed our drives. I asked why they were standing there.

"They are our 'forecaddies'—one boy for each player," he said.

By then, we were a small army of twelve people. Once on the green, and after my putt found the cup, I bent down to retrieve the ball.

"Please do not pick up your ball," my host said. "That is the 'green caddy's' job."

I learned later that they wanted to employ as many people as possible to reduce begging on the nearby city streets. Third-world golf was a unique experience.

The flight(s) to Cannes on the French Riviera took about two days, much of it waiting for the next connecting flight. From Bombay, I flew to Lahore, Pakistan on Air France, then on to Cairo, Athens, and Rome. The last leg was a short flight from Rome to Cannes.

Getting to Cannes had taken twenty hours of actual flight time on three different airlines across three time zones. Except for me and several Indian 'Bollywood' film executives, very few people were traveling from Bombay to the Cannes Film Festival.

Ed Feldman's picture *You're a Big Boy Now* didn't win any awards, but it was the first movie directed by Francis Ford Coppola. As the executive producer, Ed was his boss.

Francis proved to be a very headstrong young man. I was there when Ed gave Francis a severe dressing down and warned him to behave or he'd have a hard time getting another job in Hollywood. Of course, we know the rest of the story.

In Monte Carlo, we played roulette at the casino and went to parties with Ed and Lorraine. At one event, we met Jerry Lewis. We dined in a palatial home overlooking the Mediterranean. During our four days in Cannes, Ed and Lorraine introduced us to movie personalities, some famous and others who would become famous in the years to come.

I was exhausted, having traveled halfway around the world in the span of two weeks. I was anxious to give my report to my father concerning our new line of Fuller twist drills, made in India.

The flight home was uneventful, and we found everything at home just as we had left it. Tired but happy, we spent a quiet weekend reuniting with our kids. It had been an exciting week, but I had no idea how "exciting" the coming weeks, months, and years would be.

Chapter 25
The Week That Shook My World

On Memorial Day weekend, I was thirty-three years old with a wife, two children, and a mortgage.

Muhammad Ali was convicted of draft evasion. Jack Nicklaus won the US Open.

The life-altering events described below are seared in my memory as if they happened yesterday.

I felt something was "off" the minute I arrived back at the office on Monday morning before the long holiday weekend. Bernie Fuller was in a happy frame of mind ten days earlier when he dropped me off at New York International Airport. After some fatherly advice, we parted. Everything seemed fine.

When I got back, there was no warm welcome. No one asked about my trip, about India, or Cannes. Instead, I was met with a stony cold silence. Clearly, my father was deliberately avoiding me.

"We need to talk," I said. "I have a full report of my visit to the twist drill factory."

"Not now," he replied. "I haven't time. This afternoon I am going to the Montreal World's Fair and will be there for a few days. It will wait until I get back."

It was 9:00 a.m. and his flight was late in the afternoon. I couldn't understand why he wouldn't talk to me. Bob Johnson was silent, although I couldn't help but notice that he, too, was avoiding me.

If I started to approach my father, he would turn his back and go the other way. This was deliberate and very confusing. I had been in trouble before, but this was serious. I had no idea why my father refused to talk to me, but I would soon find out.

Miles Godin was friendly with everyone in the office, especially Bob Johnson. Bob would know why I was being ignored by my father and he would tell Miles everything. I had to talk to Miles.

Closing the door to my office, I called Miles. It didn't take him long to tell me what he knew. This what he told me.

It had not gone unnoticed when Pat and I took an expensive cruise on the SS France a few months before. Now we had gone to the Cannes Film Festival.

When I called my mother to let her know we were home, all she said to to me was, "You and your wife are jet-setting around the world as if money is no object." She was very angry, as usual.

Helen told my father that something must be done. Pat and I were living too "high on the hog" (strange phrasing for a person who claimed to be strictly kosher). Bernie must take "Buzzy" down a peg or two and teach him a lesson. Why did June have to work, and Pat didn't? My sister Dee complained that Jerry's business kept him away in England and Japan while she was stuck at home with three young boys. Why should Buzzy and Pat be allowed to take fancy cruises and trips Europe? Who did they think they were?

Bernie was getting complaints about me from my mother, my sisters, and a mystery person. He did not know what to do, so he decided to get out of town and go to Canada for the Montreal World's Fair with his lawyer, Jerry Silbert of the Proskaur law firm.

Together, they would devise a plan to punish me for my attitude and other transgressions. Until he retuned, no one in the company was permitted to talk to me.

Miles Godin was not an employee of Fuller Tool Company, and he hoped he would be safe. I went home, distraught and confused by my sudden exile and spent the weekend trying to figure out what I might have done to cause such a reaction.

Ronald Mandler was a good friend and so I asked him if he had any idea about why my father was ignoring me. Ronald had no idea but did notice that while I was away, Lillian, the company bookeeper, had been behind closed doors with my father a few times. Ronald thought it had something to do with him and the IBM machine that Lillian had refused to learn.

I, too, had become frustrated with our long-time bookeeper and the last of the original employees. Lillian insisted accounting entries should be made by hand in ledger books. Lillian knew I wanted her to retire and was probably complaining about me to my father.

After a weekend in Montreal with his lawyer, my father returned to the office. Promptly at 9:00 a.m., I was summoned to his office. The door was closed.

My father wanted to know why I had a secret bank account and said that he "knew" I was selling inventory after hours, from my car, for cash. He said he was informed that my treachery had been going on while he was away in Florida.

My father refused to listen to me or to reveal his "sources." I had no idea what he was talking about or why anyone would accuse me of such outlandish actions. I was stunned and confused, but one thing was clear: my father no longer trusted me. The questions continued.

Q. "Why did you fire the company bookeeper, Lillian Sasanow?"
A. "I didn't fire her. Lillian is in her office right now."

Q. "We know you have a 'secret' bank account?"
A. "No such account exists anywhere."

Q "You have been padding your expense accounts."
A. "Check the reports for yourself. You won't find anything wrong."

Q. "We were told you are selling Fuller Tools from your car, for cash."
A. "That's crazy! Who told you that?"

Father said, "I do not believe your denials."

He refused to hear anything I said!

Father: "If you wish to continue working here, your mother and I have decided on some new rules.

He proceeded to tell me the "New Rules."

1. "You are no longer President of Fuller Tool Company. I am once again president and Chairman of the Board, for life."

2. "I have cabled your Indian friend, Ashok Birla, and cancelled the purchase order you gave him. I told him you had no authority to commit Fuller Tool Company without my approval."

3. "You are to pay a 'fine' for stealing company merchandise and for taking unapproved vacations."

4. "Your annual compensation will be reduced."

5. "You must contribute 10 percent of your salary to the Bernard and Helen Fuller Foundation."

I replied that Fuller Tool Company was his and that I was his employee. I said, "Apparently, you do not believe me and do not trust me, so maybe I should resign.

"However, if I resign, I would like to buy or run Award Tool Company as it will give me a 'leg up' so that I can continue to support Pat and David and Susan. Award was my idea from the beginning, and I should be allowed to buy it for my future. You 'spun off' the cutlery business and created Regent Sheffield so that Jerry Hahn (my older sister's husband) could support your daughter and your three grandsons."

He said, "Okay, but first you must resign from Fuller tool Company."

At that moment, I had two choices: Door Number 1 or Door Number 2.

Door Number 1: No longer President, a reduction in salary, a fine, and other punishments, or

Door Number 2: Resign from Fuller Tool and own (or run) Award Tool Co.

I chose Door Number 2.

He simply said, "I think that would be best."

I had always believed that I would spend my working life at the family business. I had studied business administration in college, and I loved sales, package design, and factory production. Building the family business, along with my father, was my only ambition.

Bernie Fuller then summoned the entire office staff (about eighteen people) and proclaimed that I had an important announcement to make.

I simply said, "I have today resigned from Fuller Tool Company. Please wish me luck. I will surely need it."

Bernie then said, "Everyone can now go back to work."

He immediately called my mother and quietly said, "Okay, it's done." He did not add, "I hope you're happy now."

My resignation was accepted with no effort to convince me to stay.

I had resigned for three reasons.

1. I was hurt by his accusations of wrongdoing and, worse, that there was no attempt to verify if any of it was true.

2. I felt that he wanted me to leave the company and as the dutiful son, I respected his wishes.

3. He had agreed that I could continue to run, or perhaps buy, Award Tools. (details would follow)

I called Jerry Silbert for procedural advice regarding my resignation and the takeover of Award but he said he could not advise me or even talk to me because his firm represented Fuller Tool Company, not me. If I wanted legal advice, I should have my own attorney. It seemed strange, but I followed his suggestion.

David Marks, a cousin of Pat's father, Jerry Green, was a respected lawyer in New York. David Marks had been on the US legal team at the Nuremberg Trials.

After hearing the ludicrous claims against me and the new rules, David believed they were made up to force my resignation. If I resigned, the firm could avoid a potential lawsuit. Firing the president of a company under false charges would be hard to defend.

The following day, there was a meeting in Jerry Silbert's office on Park Avenue in New York City. I was not represented by my attorney.

Jerry handed me a document (on stationery from the hotel in Montreal) to sign. It was a letter from me to the chairman of the board of Fuller Tool Co. Inc. In a few words, it said that I hereby tendered my voluntary resignation from Fuller Tool Co. or words to that effect. I signed the letter, as did the chairman (i.e., my father). The attorney took the letter and in exchange handed me a check for my twelve years of service to Fuller Tool Co. I thanked him and said I would use most of the money to help finance the purchase of Award Tool Co., although it might take a while for me to pay off the balance.

Jerry Silbert demolished that fantasy. "That's not going to happen," he said. "We have given the matter a lot of thought and Award Tools is not for sale. We believe you would use Award to compete against Fuller Tool."

"That's crazy. I would not do that, and besides, Fuller Tool is the exclusive supplier of Award Tools. The purpose of taking over Award is so that I can continue to manage the company I created. I want to protect the reputation of Fuller Tool Company, not compete against Fuller Tool Company any more than Jerry Hahn would.

"Award will allow me to support my family. Besides, my father has agreed that I could take over Award Tool as a condition of my resignation."

I reminded everyone that I had created Award Tools to expand sales to discount stores while protecting the image of Fuller Tool as a major supplier to hardware distributors and traditional hardware stores. The plan succeeded and added millions of dollars in new sales and profit to its parent, Fuller Tool Company.

"Yes, and we thank you for that."

The company lawyer then said, "Purchase orders for Award Tools will be filled with Fuller Tools. Award Tool customers will be notified that the Award brand is discontinued and replaced with Fuller Tools."

It remains unforgivable that my own father conspired to "eliminate" his son, went back on his promise, and closed a successful and valuable business.

Looking back from the distance of many years, I should not have been surprised. Bernie Fuller had always been devious, weak, and therefore dangerous.

Bernie and Helen had pushed out anyone who might seem to threaten Bernie, starting with his brother, Fred Fuller. Over the years, I was followed out the door by my sister June's husband, Martin Sloan, two grandsons (Jonathan and Ari), and another brother (Marty Fuller). Jerry Hahn was ostrasized when he divorced my sister Dee.

My mother and two sisters had a quick reply to friends and relatives who would ask what happened. They said. *"Buzzy resigned because he wanted to start his own business."*

To their employees, they spread the lie that I had a "secret" bank account funded with money claimed to be "travel expenses," and that I was selling Fuller Tools from the trunk of my car after hours.

Bernie immediately resumed as President and Chairman of the Board but complained that he could not spend next winter in Florida! Too bad.

Suddenly, I was in a serious financial and emotional situation. I loved my job, and I loved the business. What happened was impossible to comprehend, especially as there was no warning.

At thirty-two, I had a wife, two kids, a mortgage, and very little in savings. The first call I made was to Pine Hollow Country Club. I asked for and received a leave of absence.

Tossing me out was a total mystery at the time, but some of the answers became clear after my father died in 2002.

Our medical insurance would soon be cut off, the company took back my car, ten years of paying into the company pension were lost, and I had a mortgage on our home in Roslyn.

I had to find another job, sell the house, or start my own business.

Chapter 26
June 1967: Unemployed

What sort of business could I create from scratch? I wanted to use my experience and connections in the hardware industry as I had no experience or connections in any other field.

My Next Enterprise

Miles Godin offered me a desk and typewriter right behind Bert Hersh, Miles's partner in the ad agency of Burton-Miles.

I accepted Miles generous offer of a free desk in his office, even though it meant taking the Long Island Railroad to New York City.

I soon conjured up a totally new and original concept: small hand tools.

Miles gave me full access to his staff of commercial artists, and I was off and running.

The concept that would soon become reality had occurred to me more than a year earlier. I was intrigued by a line of hobby tools from a small company called Pluto Tools.

Pluto was in a house in Freeport, Long Island. They had been around for many years. I knew the owner, whose name I have forgotten. He was a quiet person and a lot older than me.

Pluto preferred to call on local hardware stores and some wholesalers in downtown New York around Canal Street. His product line consisted of twelve SKUs (the term SKU, or Stock Keeping Unit, wasn't invented yet).

I remembered a one-ounce pinpoint oiler, a set of miniature files, and some precision screwdrivers. During my visit to his business the year before, I had asked "Mr. Pluto" if he was interested in selling his company to Fuller Tool Company. He declined.

The Pluto line was a good idea, but I felt it had far more potential. A much broader selection of consumer quality precision tools would emerge, fully formed in my mind. I was sure it could become a significant business. I envisioned a white (Masonite) pegboard with the best twenty-five small hand tools, all similarly packaged.

The National Hardware Show was to be held at the New York Coliseum (long since gone) in four months (October 1967). If I could show prototype samples of my new line to fifty or more hardware buyers from around the country, I would have the feedback I needed to go into business. I would source the various items from established factories in the United States to create a unified line. It was like preparing a good Caesar salad. The salad is only as good as what you include in it.

Many of the hardware distributors, co-ops, and discount store buyers I knew personally from my years at Fuller Tool Company and Award Tool Company would be at the National Hardware Show. I intended to "buttonhole" everyone I could to show my new line. I wanted to be able to tell them that Omega would be ready to deliver its initial orders in the first quarter of 1970.

First, the new company needed a name that would imply high quality. I suggested the name Omega Precision Hand Tools," but worried that people might confuse us with Omega Watch Company. Pat looked at it differently, saying, "People should associate Omega Tools with Omega watches. That's a good thing."

With the company name and logo set, I had to decide which items to include in the initial assortment. Certain tools were obvious, such as mini-pliers, precision screwdrivers, rulers, and calipers. Other products that might fit into the assortment were less well known. The "good stuff" was usually kept behind the counter, where the store owner could keep them secure.

My research consisted of visits to many hardware stores, paint stores, and hobby stores. I had to determine the best items, from many possible choices, to include in the initial Omega assortment. I asked store owners and sales clerks to bring an item or two from behind the counter. I would purchase any item I thought would be a good addition to the line.

I had envisioned a Masonite panel to display a selection of twenty-five consumer priced and packaged Omega Precision tools. Consumers, while walking through their favorite hardware stores, could see and possibly purchase an Omega product. Meanwhile, more expensive, precision instruments for professional users would remain in a locked security case that only the owner could open.

From the beginning, I wanted every Omega package to look the same as every other Omega package. This method had worked extremely well for Award Tools.

Twenty-five different but related items, all packaged alike, with several of each item per peg hook on a bright white pegboard panel would make a powerful presentation. The typical do-it-yourselfer would take a minute to stop and look.

With the initial twenty-five items determined, the creative staff at Burton-Miles Advertising proceeded to design the package.

The next steps were more complex. Fortunately, through my experience with both domestic and foreign suppliers, I had a Rolodex with the names of many potential suppliers. I knew whom to contact for each of the products I wanted in the original assortment of Omega Precision hand tools.

Beyond securing the products to package and sell, we needed factory space, an office, material handling equipment, storage racks for inventory, production tables, packaging machines, shipping supplies and, most important, workers.

Small Hand tools for hobbyists, craftsmen, and mechanics

Chapter 27
Filling in the gaps

At this point in the story, I would like to fill in some gaps not (directly) related to business. Before the summer of 1967, things were going along quite happily.

Susan and David were seven and four respectively. David started camp at Raquette Lake Boys Camp. Susan was in day camp. That left time for Pat and me to enjoy Pine Hollow. We called it our "camp for parents."

We had many good friends: Joe and Irene Draizen, Alan and Renee Hoffman, Irving and Helen Simes, and many others. We played couples golf on Sundays, and I played with the men on Saturdays. Our social life was exciting. There were casual dinners at the club. Formal attire was required on Memorial Day, Labor Day, and on New Year's Eve. We attended weddings and countless bar mitzvahs.

For a few years, I was active in club affairs and served on the board when Mike Tempkin was president. Everybody said Mike could have been a great stand-up comedian. He was smart, too.

There were trips to the Catskills, Washington, DC, and visits to our friends Roberta and Kenny Lonoff in Livingston, New Jersey. We even flew to London to attend the bar mitzvah of Ruth and Maurice Felber's son. It was a memorable (and very long) weekend.

One year, we packed up the kids in our station wagon and drove to a Disney World resort in Florida. We stayed in motels along the way. It was a family bonding trip, but with a lot of yelling and screaming. Everyone was glad to get home.

Our friend Bill Ferriter had moved back to San Francisco after he was discharged. Once home, he married his high school sweetheart. It didn't last and they were soon divorced.

Bill was an early computer programmer. In those early days, before Microsoft and Apple, Bill Gates and Steve Jobs were still in grade school. If you knew computer language like FORTRAN and could "program" IBM computers, it was easy to get a high-paying job.

Bill set up the first hospital computer system for Mt. Sinai Hospital in New York City. The job required him to be in New York for at least eight weeks.

During his stay in New York City, Bill decided that his true calling was acting, not computers. Meanwhile, as a computer programmer, he was able to support himself and an apartment, which he shared with a new girlfriend, on the West Side of New York near the Metropolitan Museum.

His girlfriend was the casting director for a very successful daytime soap opera on TV. Bill became an actor on *All My Children*.

For years after, Bill would be stopped on the street and recognized by fans wherever he went. Unfortunately, after he and the casting director broke up, his acting career came to a halt.

Eventually, he went back into computer programming, but time had passed him by and everything was different and more complicated.

I don't remember when I developed ulcerative colitis. My case is considered moderately severe. No one has yet found a cure, but UC can be treated with drugs. There are long periods of remission, followed by equally long periods of flare-ups. UC is often found among Jews of Eastern European descent.

Andy Jeffrey and Steve Gutman were my college roommates and lifelong personal friends. It is important for me to include something about each of them in this discourse.

My old college roommate, Andy Jeffrey, was a product of the 60s. Back home in New York, he couldn't find a job he liked. He joined the migration to Los Angeles and worked in the "military industrial complex," a term coined by President Eisenhower. He never said what he did, but apparently, he was very good at it. He got married, had a son, and bought a house in a nice section of Los Angeles and property in Washington state. Things were looking up.

One day, returning home early from work, he found his wife in bed with the gardener. They divorced soon after.

Later in his life, Andy found his true love and got married again. One year later, he suffered a severe stroke. He was relearning how to speak when he passed away. Andy was sixty-eight years old and the first of my close friends to die.

My other college roommate at Lehigh, Steve Gutman, started his postgraduate career on Wall Street as an analyst with Merrill Lynch. He rose quickly and after a few years, was offered a senior management position with another Wall Street firm.

Steve had a good friend who was the personal accountant to Leon Hess owner of Hess Oil and the New York Jets football team.

His friend told Steve that Mr. Hess was interviewing prospects for business manager for the Jets. An interview with Steve was soon arranged and, after three more interviews, Steve got the job!

Within two years, Steve Gutman was made president of the New York Jets.

For the next twenty seasons, Pat and I, at the invitation of Steve and his vivacious wife Carol, enjoyed watching the Jets from the president's suite.

In August 1967, the United States sent 45,000 troops to Vietnam. A nuclear bomb was tested in Nevada desert. Thurgood Marshall became the first black justice of US Supreme Court.

Chapterf 28
Brick and Mortar

In August 1967, Omega rented factory space in College Point, Queens. It was 3,000 square feet with eighteen-foot ceilings and two bathrooms, but no office.

We hired a carpenter to construct an office and purchased a couple of second-hand desks and two used file cabinets for fifteen dollars (one for accounts receivable and one for accounts payable). Over a weekend, Pat and I painted the office ourselves. From home, we brought in a coffee maker and Pat's portable typewriter for billing.

While we waited for the first products to arrive and for our color catalog to be printed, there was a mountain of work to do.

At the end of December 1969, five months after the company was conceived and just six months after I left Fuller Tool Company, Omega Precision Hand Tools shipped its very first customer purchase order.

Within two weeks, I received a call from a distributor in Boston. The initial twenty assortments (number 100A) had completely sold out and they needed another fifty assortments shipped as soon as possible. They also needed additional open stock to refill empty hooks on assortments sold to hardware stores.

With confidence, I began hiring sales agents to cover the Eastern seaboard from Maine to Miami and west to Pittsburgh. Each salesman received a full-size sample of assortment 100A with all twenty-five items glued to the panel. Each also received a supply of full-color catalog pages and order forms.

The reception to our line, although it was a new concept, was an immediate hit. Virtually every hardware wholesaler wanted to buy our line. We were an "overnight" success.

There was one problem. Omega was burning cash faster than it came in. During our first year, we had to build up our inventory to be able to fill customer orders fast enough. Although the company was new, most of our suppliers agreed to thirty-day payment terms instead of cash on delivery. Our customers, meanwhile, paid in thirty days, and often longer. Our cash flow became negative very quickly. We needed a cash infusion quickly.

Fortunately, I had developed a good relationship with the manager of our local Chase Manhattan branch. Over five years, I had negotiated bank loans for Fuller Tool Company and Award Tool. Every loan had been paid back on time.

Of course, Omega had no track record, no credit history, or sufficient inventory and receivables, so the bank required my personal guarantee. Although it was risky, Omega needed working capital. I signed the personal guarantee. Between long-term bank loans and good supplier terms, we managed to finance our rapid growth.

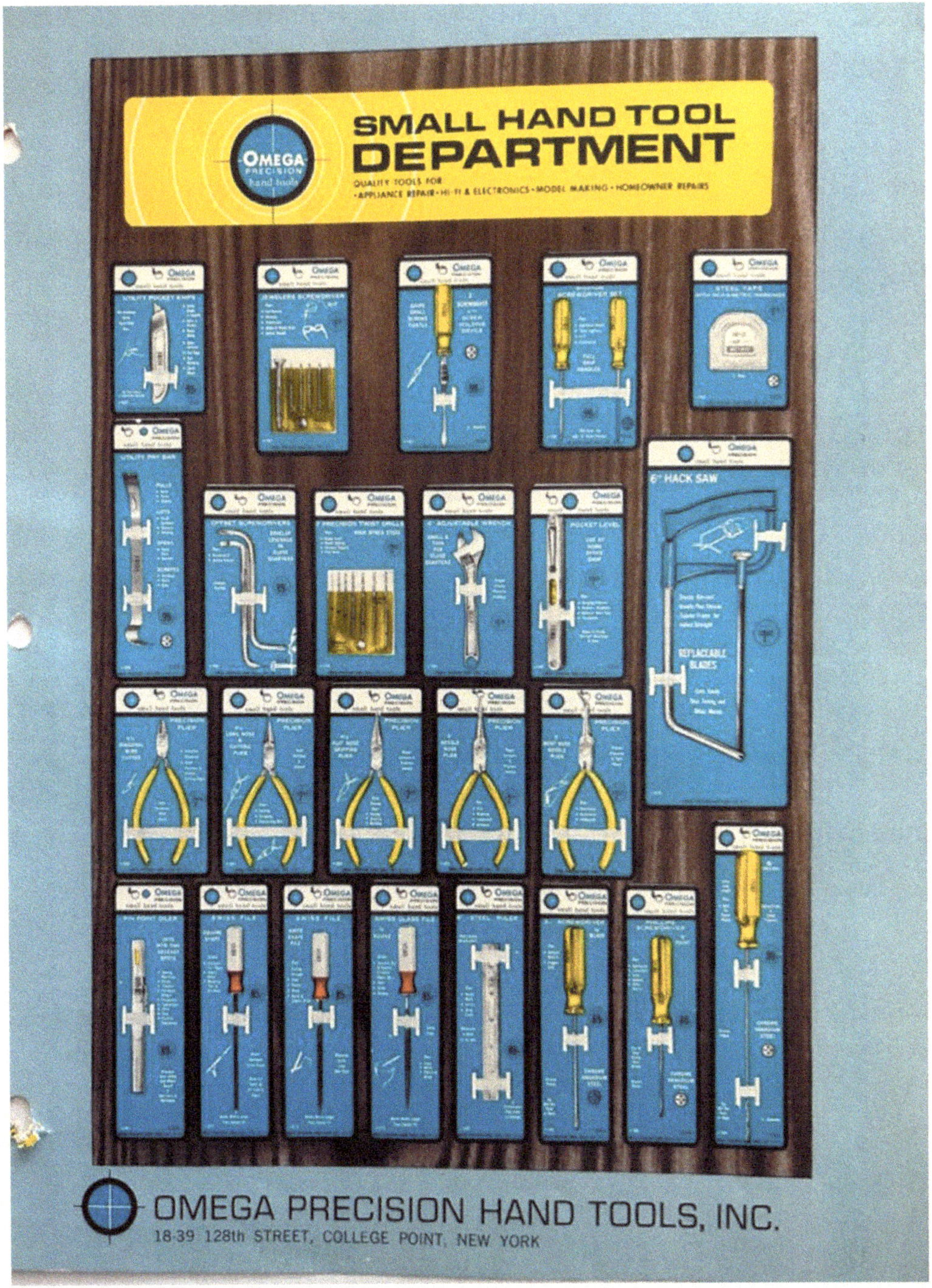
SMALL HAND TOOL
DEPARTMENT
OMEGA
PRECISION
hand tools
QUALITY TOOLS FOR
•APPLIANCE REPAIR•HI-FI & ELECTRONICS•MODEL MAKING•HOMEOWNER REPAIRS
6" HACK SAW
REPLACEABLE BLADES
OMEGA PRECISION HAND TOOLS, INC.
18-39 128th STREET, COLLEGE POINT, NEW YORK

True Value Hardware was created by John Cotter just before the outbreak of World War 2. It was the first hardware co-op in the United States. Cotter wanted to build a national co-op along the lines of the successful dairy farm co-ops.

By the early 1960s, True Value Hardware and ACE Hardware represented 12,000 neighborhood hardware stores, across the country. Another 30,000 hardware stores were supplied by local wholesalers.

If I could land True Value and/or ACE Hardware, Omega Tools would be universally recognized by the hardware industry as a successful brand of (small) hand tools.

John's son, Dan Cotter, was the same age as me and was the new tool buyer for True Value Hardware. Dan and I had a lot in common. We were both sons of successful businessmen and had grown up in the family business. We liked and respected each other.

Danny had heard the stories about how I had left Fuller Tool Company and that I had recently started my own company. He wanted to hear all about it.

I left my initial meeting with Dan Cotter with a confirmed True Value warehouse order for 1,000 displays of assortment 100A and sufficient open stock inventory to cover all refill requirements for at least the next three months.

This was the boost the company needed. From then on, we had no trouble selling our new product line to virtually every hardware distributor with a good credit rating.

The success of Omega did not go unnoticed by other hand tool companies including, Fuller Tool Company, Great Neck Saw, General Hardware, and Evans Rule Company.

PRECISION MEASURING INSTRUMENTS

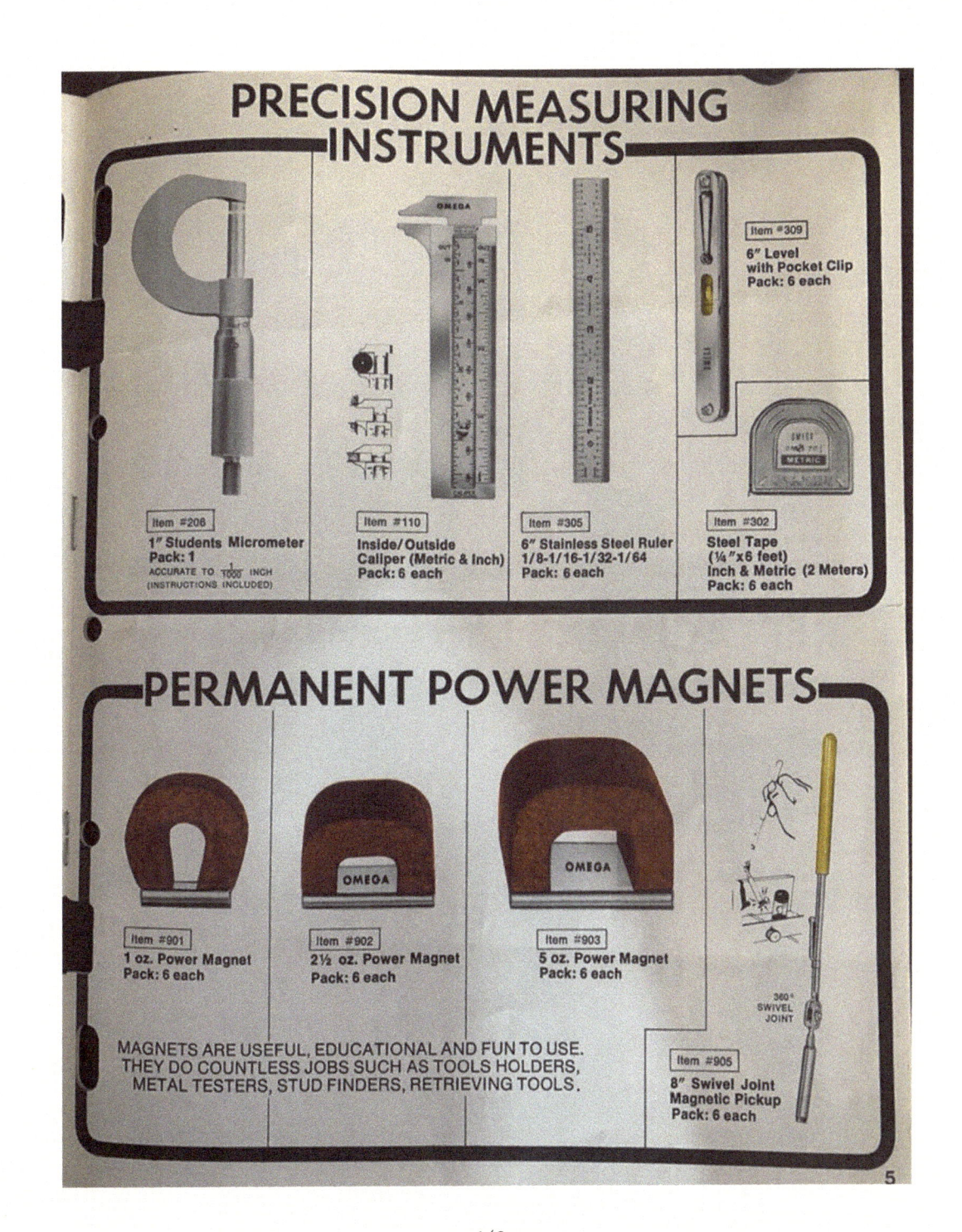

Item #206
1" Students Micrometer
Pack: 1
ACCURATE TO 1/1000 INCH
(INSTRUCTIONS INCLUDED)

Item #110
Inside/Outside Caliper (Metric & Inch)
Pack: 6 each

Item #305
6" Stainless Steel Ruler
1/8-1/16-1/32-1/64
Pack: 6 each

Item #309
6" Level with Pocket Clip
Pack: 6 each

Item #302
Steel Tape (¼"x 6 feet)
Inch & Metric (2 Meters)
Pack: 6 each

PERMANENT POWER MAGNETS

Item #901
1 oz. Power Magnet
Pack: 6 each

Item #902
2½ oz. Power Magnet
Pack: 6 each

Item #903
5 oz. Power Magnet
Pack: 6 each

Item #905
8" Swivel Joint Magnetic Pickup
Pack: 6 each

360° SWIVEL JOINT

MAGNETS ARE USEFUL, EDUCATIONAL AND FUN TO USE. THEY DO COUNTLESS JOBS SUCH AS TOOLS HOLDERS, METAL TESTERS, STUD FINDERS, RETRIEVING TOOLS.

5

I knew the owners of each of these companies and realized they all were far larger than Omega. If they wanted to, they could undersell me on many items and could critically damage my young business.

To avoid potential competitors, I approached Great Neck Saw and General Hardware as potential suppliers. Both had several products that would fit nicely into the Omega line.

I purchased a mini utility knife from Evans Rule and from Great Neck Saw a mini hacksaw and a six-inch level. General Hardware provided a small caliper, a micrometer, and several sizes of magnets. Every supplier agreed to imprint Omega on the items they supplied. Potential competitors were neutralized—except for Fuller Tool Company.

Chapter 29
Lesson Learned

When I left Fuller Tool Company in 1967, I took a leave of absence from Pine Hollow Country Club. Eventually, Omega was doing well enough, and I rejoined the club.

We met Joe and Irene Drazin, who were in their sixties while Pat and I were in our forties.

Joe Draizin was outgoing and especially good with young kids. He invited Susan and David to the judo class he ran every Tuesday evening at Temple Beth Sholem in Roslyn.

Judo training was good for both kids, but Susan enjoyed the classes more than David and became quite skilled.

One day, an older boy wielding a broomstick was taunting David. Susan jumped between them and took an offensive judo position. Susan was prepared to take down her brother's attacker using the judo skills she had learned in class. The other kid was so intimidated, he dropped the broom handle and ran home.

Joe was in the ladies' millinery business. At about the time we became friends, ladies' hats were already starting to go out of fashion. Sales were way off and Joe found himself desperately short of cash. At that point, he made a serious mistake that would quickly destroy his business and put him in legal jeopardy.

To generate extra cash, he delayed remitting his employee's deductions of federal taxes and Social Security.

It wasn't long before the IRS padlocked his factory door and ordered him to immediately remit the amount due with interest or face serious legal action. I loaned him money to pay the IRS.

Joe paid the loan back, but his company never recovered and soon closed. They sold their home in Roslyn and moved to Florida.

CHAPTER 30
Growing the Business

Omega was doing well enough to hire a full-time sales manager. Joe Cafferella was energetic, young, and single. He had the experience and qualifications for the job. With Joe C. on board, we didn't need most of the independent sales reps we were using.

Before we let a rep go, Joe suggested that he travel with him for five days. He could then decide who to let go and who to retain. Most were let go.

With a company sales manager, our sales costs were lowered. Our actual sales, however, stayed about the same. The economy was in the midst of rampant inflation. Every six months, we had to raise some prices. After another six months, we would raise prices on products not raised before.

In addition to runaway inflation, interest rates kept rising. Before the end of the 70s, interest rates would climb above 15 percent. Everyone was struggling to stay profitable as the cost of goods and the cost of financing were getting out of control.

One solution that would lower our cost of goods was to reduce the number of items made in the United States and replace them with the same items produced and fully packaged overseas. The net result would be a significant cost savings. I had to find out if this strategy was possible.

In September 1971, six Ku Klux Klan members were arrested for bombing ten school buses. Chris Evert won her first US Open tennis tournament. Watergate burglars raided Daniel Elsberg's office.

In September of 1971, I made my first trip for Omega to Japan. I was met by a Japanese agent with whom I had corresponded at the recommendation of one of his American clients.

Tetsura Iwabi was a very pleasant fellow, well-educated, and polite. He had arranged for me to visit three cities and ten factories in five days, all within driving distance.

Before starting out, we spoke for over four hours so that he would know exactly what I was looking for. I would learn if he was the right man for the job. He was.

I was in good hands. The factories he had lined up to visit were modern and efficient. Tetsura would be required to inspect and approve the finished products before shipment.

He would consolidate the production of several factories into a single container. When it was ready, he would reserve space on a fast vessel to New York.

Tetsura's work ethic, knowledge, and honesty were invaluable to Omega. As compensation, Tetsura would earn 5 percent of the factory cost. This was what he requested, and I readily agreed.

Over time, we added several new products: a lighted magnifier, a pinpoint oiler and six-inch stainless-steel ruler made in California.

We also added a new salesman for national accounts. Ron Smiley had joined our company with a strong background in sales to large national accounts. Ron would "wine and dine" a buyer until he or she gave him a purchase order. He enjoyed traveling and attending trade shows. As a result, our business continued to expand.

On February 5, 1974, Patricia Hearst, nineteen-year-old daughter of publisher Randolph Hearst, was kidnapped by the Symbionese Liberation Army. Richard M. Nixon announced that he would resign. Vice President Gerald R. Ford was sworn in as the thirty-eighth President of the United States on August 9. Ford granted a "full, free, and absolute pardon" to former president Nixon on September 8.

CHAPTER 31
TRUE VALUE HARDWARE

By January 1974, we had been a True Value vendor for four years. Our products were successfully carried by most of their members and frequently appeared in promotional flyers distributed by individual dealers.

Bernie Zurn, the tool buyer, had been considering a house brand of hand tools that they could purchase and sell at lower prices than the big American brands, such as Stanley Tools, Nicholson Files, and Estwing Hammers. The exclusive house brand would consist of a full range of hand tools and be sold in all six-thousand-member stores. Every tool would show the brand name of Servess.

Bernie wanted to introduce the new Servess brand as a "tool of the month" national promotion. He decided it would be a fourteen-inch Servess pipe wrench sold at a "door buster" retail price. All True Value retailers would participate. The smallest dealers could order as few as twelve pipe wrenches. Larger stores would order up to 120 each. With six thousand True Value stores in the United States, Mexico, and Canada, the company would require the vendor, by contract, to deliver 250,000 pipe wrenches by a certain date. As a national promotion, True Value would run newspaper ads, radio spots, and the first True Value television commercial.

Bernie had wanted Rigid Pipe Wrench Company to fill the promotion order, but they declined. He then sought out other manufacturers, including Fuller Tool Company, but everyone turned him down. No American company wanted to sell their products under a private label at a lower price.

Bernie Zurn asked us if I had any suggestions. I told him that I knew the largest manufacturer of pipe wrenches in Europe and the owner, Juan Luis Aguirre, was a supplier and a friend.

If he wanted, I would ask Juan Luis if his company, Ego Tools, could fill an order for 250,000 pipe wrenches by the delivery date and at the price required. Bernie Zurn said he needed to know quickly, or the tool of the month promotion would be cancelled. As it was his idea, it would reflect very badly on him. Would I do my best?

I called Juan Luis. He would need to consult with his production people and accountants before making a commitment. I had called him on a Friday. He promised to cable his reply on the following Monday.

I told Juan Luis that each tool must have the Servess name and logo. He was fine with that as his pipe wrenches were already sold under various private brand names in countries beyond Spain.

Finally, on Monday morning, I got the call. The factory could meet the deadline for delivery and the price. Every tool would have the Servess name and logo.

I called Bernie Zurn and gave him the good news.

That same day by Telex, Omega received a purchase order from True Value Hardware for 250,000 Servess fourteen-inch pipe wrenches to be delivered at the price and by the date indicated.

It was by far the largest and most important purchase order we had ever received. It would also be a major challenge.

I immediately booked a flight to Madrid then to Eibar in northern Spain. At the time, there was a bitter fight going on between the Basques in Northern Spain and border villages in France. The Basque region wanted independence from the Franco-led government in Madrid. The Basque people had their own language and traditions as a mountain people, which differed from that of most of Spain. Before World War 2, Franco had succeeded, with the support of the Germans and Italians, to defeat the Republican government. In 1939, Franco had bombed the city of Guernica in the Basque region. Pablo Picasso memorialized this tragic event that killed thousands of civilians in a painting called simply *Guernica*.

Juan Aguirre met me at the Bilbao airport for the fifty-mile drive through the mountains to the industrial city of Eibar, where his pipe wrench factory was located. The road was blockaded at checkpoints manned by government soldiers with automatic weapons at the ready. My US passport was honored, and I had no problem. Juan, however, was ordered to step outside the car. He was subjected to body searches for concealed weapons. His identity card was taken for confirmation and only returned after ten minutes. After we reached Eibar, we encountered roadblocks manned by Basque separatists at barricades of burning tires. I began to worry whether the factory could operate in an atmosphere of distrust and potential violence.

Juan assured me that the central government needed the industrial production of the Basque provinces. The Basques not only produced coal, iron ore, and steel but their exports provided hard currency, especially US dollars and German marks.

The next day, we toured a modern factory. It had been rebuilt after it was bombed by Franco during the Spanish Civil War, only to be rebuilt to provide weapons to Nazi Germany and fascist Italy. After the war, they rebuilt it again to export hand tools for the recovery of Europe. Until my visit, they had never exported to the United States, and they were very excited to do so.

To proceed, there were pre-conditions to the contract.

1. The product would meet the provided US federal specifications.

2. Under no circumstances would the final price be renegotiated.

3. The due date for delivery in Chicago will not be extended, under penalty of cancellation and non-payment.

4. If the merchandise was refused due to late delivery or noncompliance with US quality standards, the factory must destroy all finished product bearing the proprietary brand name of Servess.

Juan Luis signed the contract.

After enjoying the world-famous cuisine of the Basque region, I flew back to Madrid to connect with my TWA flight to New York.

The lead time for production and final delivery was five months. The order was placed on January 20 for arrival in Chicago no later than June 20, 1974. The transit time for ocean freight from Spain to New York was four weeks. Another week would be needed for it to arrive by rail car in Chicago. To be safe, we added two weeks from arrival in New York. This proved to be a fortuitous decision.

Right on schedule, two containers containing 250,000 fourteen-inch pipe wrenches departed the port of Bilbao en route to the port of New York. The ship picked up additional cargo in Marseille, Southampton, and Newfoundland, Canada. Our two containers should arrive in New York in thirty days.

A potential disaster was in the making just as our two containers departed Bilbao, Spain.

The Longshoremen's Union went out on strike. All arriving vessels were suddenly denied entry into the port of New York. Nothing would move in or out during the strike. There was no way to guess how long it might last. Our container ship was already on its way to its first stop in Newfoundland, Canada.

As soon as I received news that the port of New York was closed, I got a call from Bernie Zurn. He expressed both doubt and fear. He also conveyed the unmistakable threat that if his tool of the month promotion was cancelled (for whatever reason), both his career and any future business between Omega Tools and the six thousand True Value hardware stores would be over.

Fortunately, I had a very good customs broker. Penson and Company had required the Spanish factory to use the fastest and most reliable steamship company.

When the longshoremen's strike was announced, Penson immediately contacted the steamship company and arranged for our two containers to be off-loaded in Newfoundland, Canada. From there, our containers could be loaded on to a barge that sailed the St. Lawrence Seaway, through the Great Lakes, to the port of Chicago.

It was complicated. A lot could have still gone wrong but didn't.

Right on time, our containers were unloaded at the True Value warehouse in Chicago, a full week before the due date.

Bernie Zurn wanted to know how I did it despite the New York dock strike. The answer was good planning, good people, and good luck. The Tool of the Month was a huge success, and I was now the "golden boy" at True Value headquarters.

To commemorate the successful event, I commissioned an oil painting of a fourteen-inch Servess brand pipe wrench, along with a True Value mechanic's toolbox.

When it was completed, I personally presented the painting to Dan Cotter, president of Cotter and Company, his father John Cotter, Chairman of the Board, and Bernie Zurn, the buyer.

A copper plaque beneath the painting said

> Presented to True Value® Hardware Company
> by Omega Precision Hand Tools Inc.
> In recognition of the largest True Value®
> "Tool of the Month" sale, June 1975
> 250,000 14" pipe wrenches

The painting would hang in the main lobby of True Value stores for many years, and eventually in the home library of John Cotter.

After the presentation, Dan Cotter took me aside and asked me if I would provide them with a continuing supply of a full range of Omega pipe wrenches exclusively for True Value members.

He said, "Many of our dealers are asking when we will stock the other sizes of pipe wrenches from ten inches to forty-eight inches."

He had caught me off guard. I was expecting another tool of the month promotion. This was much bigger by far.

I thanked him for the opportunity but told him I would need help in financing such large quantities. Dan Cotter immediately offered to provide Omega with a revolving letter of credit. With a revolving letter of credit from Cotter and Company, any bank would be happy to lend me whatever I needed. We shook hands and I accepted his offer.

Back in his office to discuss the details, Bernie Zurn suddenly asked me, "How does it feel to be a rich man?" I could not answer; my head was still spinning.

Within a week, we received a confirming purchase order. We were required to ship four sizes of Servess brand pipe wrenches to each of their five distribution centers located around the United States. The distribution centers would accept the initial stock to support each store in their area, based on the size of each store.

In addition, all five distribution centers were required to hold sufficient back-up inventory for three months of estimated sales.

This opening order to fill the entire True Value pipeline was far larger than the 250,000 wrenches required for their tool of the month promotion.

Fortunately, this opening order would bypass our warehouse and be delivered from the port of New York, then via rail to each of their five distribution centers. In addition, we would be paid as soon as the goods were accepted by the steamship company.

Future deliveries would be held in our New York warehouse, pending specific orders to deliver to each True Value warehouse.

This presented us with a problem. If our business continued to expand, we would need more space than we had in College Point.

We found a suitable building in New Hyde Park just below Hillside Avenue and five minutes from my house. There was sufficient office space for me to have my own office. My secretary had the adjacent office. I even hired a professional office decorator.

The new facility had an eighteen-foot ceiling and could accommodate steel racks to hold over one hundred pallets of merchandise. I signed a very favorable lease as my new landlord was a personal friend from Pine Hollow Country Club.

Once everything was operational, we held a factory warming party for thirty friends, suppliers, and co-workers. It was a wonderful event. It felt like the future had arrived. In the fall of 1974, I was forty years old.

Using the high volume of True Value warehouse orders and the prompt payment provided by their letters of credit, we convinced Juan Luis to produce Omega brand pipe wreches at the same low price negotiated for 250,000 Servess pipe wrenches.

This was the same tactic used by Fuller Tools. Whenever Sears Roebuck purchased a new product from Fuller Tool Company under the new Sears Brand, Fuller would add the same item to its own line at the same low cost negotiated for the much higher quantity of Sears brand hand tools sold in Sears Roebuck megastores.

Ron Smiley and Joe Cafferella were able to sell a professional quality line of Omega pipe wrenches at very competitive consumer prices.

Of course, this decision put us in direct competition with Fuller Tool Company and several other manufacturers and importers of full-size hand tools.

Bernie Zurn continued to expand the Servess line. In short order, they added adjustable wrenches, files from Portugal, and cutting pliers, all supplied by Omega Tools. The products and orders for Servess tools were determined in Chicago. The prices and factories, whether in Europe or the East, were my responsibility.

ServEss

Ass't. No. 9850SD
Chisel Assortment

3 fast selling chisels (½" - ¾" - 1") and 3 piece chisel set. Forged steel, ground sharp edges. Complete with colorful Servess backdrop and all hooks.

ASSORTMENT NO. 9850SD CONTAINS:

Cotter Warehouse IBM No.	Omega No.	Description	Assmt. Contains (Each)	Reorder Pack
129684	982S	½" Drop Forged Wood Chisel	5	5
131136	983S	¾" Drop Forged Wood Chisel	5	5
132100	984S	1" Drop Forged Wood Chisel	5	5
132118	985S	3 Pc. Drop Forged Wood Chisel Set	3	5

Ass't. No. 6000SD
Adjustable Wrenches

4 popular adjustable wrenches with vinyl grips. Drop forged, polished and chrome plated. Complete with colorful Servess backdrop and all hooks.

ASSORTMENT NO. 6000SD CONTAINS:

Cotter Warehouse IBM No.	Omega No.	Description	Assmt. Contains (Each)	Reorder Pack
126623	606S	6" Adjustable Wrench	4	5
126631	608S	8" Adjustable Wrench	4	5
126649	610S	10" Adjustable Wrench	4	5
126656	612S	12" Adjustable Wrench	2	5

POLICY "A" STATEMENT:
If a Servess Tool does not give user complete satisfaction, it will be replaced free of charge.

True Value HARDWARE STORES — Manufactured for True Value Hardware Stores/Headquarters Chicago Ill. 60614

As we did with pipe wrenches, each time True Value added a new item as a Servess brand hand tool, the factory would produce a smaller quantity branded Omega. We soon could offer a wide range of the most popular types and sizes of standard size hand tools.

Miles-Godin designed the packaging and the sales material used by our distributors to sell Omega tools to their hardware stores.

At the time, there were about 25,000 independent mom and pop hardware stores supplied by about 400 hardware distributors in the United States. About half of them bought and sold Omega Precision Tools. That was not bad for a company in business only five years.

Now that we had expanded our product line into full-size hand tools, we found the going was a lot tougher. I had always said you would be known for your first successful product line, which in our case was smaller versions of standard hand tools, sometimes called "kitchen drawer" tools and true precision tools for hobbyists and craftsmen.

When we entered the big leagues with a line of full-size hand tools, we encountered competition. However, annual sales were exceeding three million dollars per year, with a good cash flow.

CHAPTER 32
Family

Fuller Tool Company now saw Omega as a threat and began a national campaign to discredit the quality of Omega tools.

The first shot was fired when my father, on the letterhead of Fuller Tool Company, sent a letter to every hardware distributor in the United States. His message was that cheap Korean cutting pliers were appearing in hardware stores. It stated that Korean made hand tools were made of low-quality steel that was prone to fail. It was obvious to everyone that he was referring to Omega mini pliers, which we made in Korea. Several customers sent me a copy of his letter with a note that they had no quality issues with our products, and one customer even offered to testify if I wanted to sue (I didn't).

The offensive letter led to a reprisal, which I later regretted.

My niece Caroline, the daughter of my younger sister June, was to be bat mitzvah in a few weeks and our family was invited. Pat and Susan could not attend, but David and I accepted. David was about fifteen at the time. I had the offensive letter written by Fuller Tool Company in my pocket. I was ready to confront my father with it after the service.

During the bat mitzvah service and with no prior notice, David was suddenly called to the *bima* (podium) to recite one of the required prayers.

An *alyah* (calling up) is considered an honor. David was stunned. He had no warning and was not prepared to recite the prayer, in Hebrew no less.

I told David to stay in his seat. At that moment, it seemed obvious, at least to me, that my mother wanted everyone to think we were all just one big happy family. I would have none of it. David, of course, was confused, having to choose between the rabbi's call and his own father telling him to stay seated. By now, the congregation and the rabbi realized that David was not going to accept the alyah. He called another name. The gauntlet had been thrown.

After the service, some people (not relatives) asked David and me why David had not gone up when called to the podium.

The truth would only confuse those who had no knowledge of a dispute between me and the family. We could only lie and say David had a sore throat and quickly changed the subject.

What I did at the bat mitzvah was wrong. I should not have disturbed the service and spurned what might have been an olive branch from them. I certainly should not have involved David. I was angry and no good decisions are made in anger. From a practical point of view, the opportunity to mend fences with my parents (and sisters) was lost, possibly forever. To no avail, the next day I apologized for my behavior. I explained that my action was my response to the nasty letter sent to my customers with the clear intention of damaging my reputation and my young business. At least the smear campaign was stopped in its tracks.

Chapter 33
Health Issues

During this time, my health was pretty good. The only problem was daily bouts with UC. People with this disease know where the restrooms are in supermarkets and other places. If they don't, it could be embarrassing.

As I had been complaining of cramps and other unpleasant digestive symptoms for some time, my primary care physician Larry Janoff ordered X-rays of my entire intestinal system. After the radiologist took the X-rays, I got dressed. As I prepared to go home, he requested that I wait a few minutes before leaving.

He quickly returned and said there was something on my X-ray that required the immediate attention of a urologist, Dr. Mike Freund. (I knew Mike since we were friends in high school.) I was instructed to drive directly to Mike's office. When I arrived, Mike was expecting me. He took the large envelope containing the X-rays and asked me to wait a few minutes. In less than five minutes, he called me in to his office. Of course, it did not escape me that something serious was going on, but I had assumed it had something to do with my digestive system. Mike was a urologist, so I was confused I and told him so.

The scan pictures were up on the viewer. Mike pointed to my right kidney. It looked fine. Then he identified my left kidney. It appeared to be hidden behind a white cloud.

"What's that white cloud?" I asked.

Mike said the white cloud was a tumor, and it was as big as a grapefruit. "This tumor has to be surgically removed," he stated. There was no doubt, and no need for a second opinion.

Probably because I had known Mike as a friend and knew that he was highly regarded in his field, I felt completely calm. It was as if he told me I had a cold, and nothing more serious. I would find out that it was very serious.

The surgery was scheduled for two weeks later. It would have been done sooner except that I had planned a business trip to California. The appointments had been made, the airline tickets purchased, and the hotel reservations confirmed. Besides, I did not know how long after the surgery I would have to wait if the trip was cancelled. I decided I would go to California and have the surgery immediately on my return. Meanwhile, I was comfortable with my decision and felt perfectly healthy.

When I got back from my trip, I entered North Shore Hospital for a radical left nephrectomy (removal of the left kidney). Mike told me that the tumor had wrapped itself around the kidney so that no part of it could be saved. A partial nephrectomy was not possible in my case.

Recovery was very long and painful as the abdominal wall had been opened. Microsurgery was not introduced until 1983. In four weeks, I was up and about and returned to work. There were no obvious effects as the human body functions quite well with only one kidney. One question remained: was the kidney tumor malignant or benign? The lab would not be able to provide the answer for six weeks. When the report came back, it was good news. The tumor was a hematoma and totally benign. Still, it had to be removed as it had wrapped itself around my kidney.

Since then, I have been under the regular care of a nephrologist. The remaining kidney has suffered under the strain of doing the job of two kidneys for more than thirty-three years. As a result, I now have third-stage kidney disease. Stage five requires dialysis.

My current doctor is optimistic, but it depends on my life span. Eventually, I will need dialysis, unless I don't live that long.

Chapter 34
Back to Business

I needed a buying agent in Taiwan. Most importers at that time used large trading companies as buying agents. However, I prefer an experienced individual person I could trust to work in the best interests of our company. This could be assured by paying a generous commission.

Trading companies were known to indulge in "double dipping." This was the practice of charging the buyers a 5 percent buying commission and a sales commission of 5 percent or more from the factory.

After several interviews, I decided on the man I wanted to represent our interests in Korea. His name in English was Lawrence or Larry. Larry was about thirty years old and married with one child. He had a degree in metallurgy but found it difficult to earn a living in his specialty.

Lawrence had a good appearance, spoke English very well, and had an engaging personality. He also was well-known to the hand tool manufacturers in in Korea as had worked for the Korean export agency as a quality control examiner for hand tools.

Within one week, Lawrence introduced me to the best sources of cutting pliers and wrenches in South Korea. At the time, the industry was in the early stages of development. The quality of hand tools was not quite up to "made in USA" pliers, but they did meet standard US specifications and compared well to the same items made in Japan.

With Larry's assurance that he would personally advise and oversee every aspect of production, I placed our initial purchase orders. In addition, the government of South Korea provided generous financial incentives to companies to export their products. US companies were favored as they were paid in dollars.

Taiwan became another important source for items in our rapidly expanding line of full-size hand tools. Open-end wrenches, closed-end wrenches, several hammers, pipe cutters, large bolt cutters and vice grip pliers rounded out the line.

Meanwhile, we increased our original line of Omega precision tools from Japan. We added more jeweler's screwdrivers, stainless steel pliers, and other precision products. The original assortment of twenty-five small hand tools had grown to fifty-five units. Still, we were always on the lookout for more.

While in Korea, I experienced the most penetrating cold weather in my life. Although the President Hotel was the best hotel in Seoul, they were chronically short of heat. The guest rooms were unheated after 11:00 p.m. and the blankets were too thin. During the day, most offices remained unheated except for a kerosene heater in the middle of the room. As a result, even during meetings, I never removed my woolen overcoat. After Korea, I rearranged my flight home to include a three-day stopover in Hawaii. I wanted to sit in the warm sun on a beach until the chill in my bones would disappear.

In 1976, Air France and British Airways began the first regularly scheduled commercial supersonic transport (SST) flights. Viking I landed on Mars. Richard Leakey discovered a 1.5 million year-old Homo erectus skull in Kenya.

In 1976, Pat and I traveled to Japan, Korea, and Taiwan on a two-week combination business and vacation trip.

Our first stop was Tokyo. We stayed at a traditional Japanese hotel and slept on tatami mats on the floor. The highlight of our visit was spending time with Pat's cousin Norman Green and his wife Vicki.

Norman and Vicki owned a beautiful house in Tokyo. Norman Green was born and raised in Brooklyn before World War 2. He served in France during the war. Norman's first job after the war was with Wyeth, the pharmaceutical company. The work required him to live in several countries in the Far East. Norman and Vicki have made Tokyo their home since the 1960s.

Norman's wife Vicki was born in Philadelphia. Every few years, they would come to the US to visit Vicki's family. Their son Jesse went to school in the US.

The Greens showed us the sights of Tokyo. Pat bought several antique mitzuki while there, which she later made into a necklace.

From Tokyo, we traveled by bullet train to the old city of Kyoto. Then, to the industrial city of Osaka, where our agent Mr. Iwabi invited us for dinner at his home. We met his wife, his children, and his mother-in-law. They all lived together in a small house with screens separating the rooms. Mrs. Iwabi prepared and served a traditional Japanese dinner, which we enjoyed, although it was difficult to eat sitting on the floor.

The next day with Mr. Iwabi, we visited and conferred with several factories that were producing quality products for Omega Tools.

By then, most hardware distributors carried Omega Tools. We also had a large following among discount stores throughout the country. Sales volume was headed toward five million dollars annually.

CHAPTER 35
Business and Pleasure

In 1975, Pat and I traveled to Northern Spain to inspect three potentially new sources for our expanding line. We were wined and dined by the factory owners much as we were during our visits to Japan, Taiwan, and Korea.

From Bilbao, we flew on to Athens, where we boarded a ship for a cruise of the Greek islands. The weather was perfect, as were the islands, the culture, and the food. The only problem was that Pat was sick for nine of the ten days aboard ship. I promised her a return trip one day. Sadly, it never happened.

An agreement between the United States and Iran freed fifty-two hostages held in Teheran since 1979.

Egyptian president Anwar el-Sadat was assassinated.

I thought it would be fun to own a house in Florida. We had vacationed in Boca Raton several times, but the trend among our friends was to own a place that you could return to every winter or whenever you wanted to. The winters in New York cold and bleak.

Boca Woods is a private community with two golf courses. Almost all the homes had already been sold, but there was a small property next to a short par 3 that could accommodate a two-bedroom ranch. We decided it was a good location for our new vacation house.

It took several months to build, but by Christmas, the house was ready. We spent most of the winter shopping. The house needed everything from kitchen supplies to patio furniture.

It soon became apparent that the house was too small. The living room had a vaulted ceiling, which wasn't very inviting, and the den was tiny. Even the pool was too small. There were some good features, like the screened-in patio. However, the house never felt quite right. After making some expensive improvements and using it just for two seasons, we sold it.

During the administration of Ronald Reagan, bank interest had blown up to 19 percent.

The usual and customary payment terms in the industry allowed for a 2 percent discount if the invoice was paid in thirty days. True Value began to extend payments to sixty days less a 2 percent discount. If a small account did that, we would not sell to them, but True Value represented more than half of all sales.

We were forced to take on additional bank loans at these high interest rates and secured by my personal gurantee. When a loan became due, it was extended. As a result, between our bank debt and very high interest rates, our profit margins became paper thin.

Chapter 36
Too close for comfort

Bernie Zurn called one day and told me that he wanted to visit our factories in Korea, which by then had become our largest supplier of Servess brand hand tools. I had to agree, although there was always a risk when your largest customer wanted to visit your largest vendors. Despite my misgivings, there was nothing I could do. I set up meetings with several of our Korean factories

Bernie Zurn and I would travel separately to Seoul, South Korea. He would fly from Chicago I would fly from New York. My agent would meet us both at Seoul International for the three-hour drive to Pusan where our primary factories were located.

When we arrived at the factory, there was a huge banner announcing

>Welcome Mr. Bernie Zurn and
>True Value Hardware Company

It was very impressive, but I was their customer. I recall having doubts about agreeing to bringing my biggest customer to meet my biggest supplier. A lot might go wrong.

Mr. Zurn, along with the factory owner, my agent, and I started a long tour of the factory. Mr. Zurn had many questions about the manufacturing process. He started with the grade and type of steel used, the weight of the forging machine, and about polishing and grinding, among others. He even wanted to know about production capacity. It took about three hours to complete the tour and for the owner to answer his questions as he was writing it all down in his notebook.

It occurred to me that he was asking the same questions I had when I first came to visit the same facility. The difference was that as a potential customer, I needed to know about forging, tempering steel, polishing, quality control, and so forth to be sure they could meet our need for quality and capacity

The owner was treating Mr. Zurn as if he were a prospective new customer. I had a bad feeling that there might have been some prior contact between the factory and Mr. Zurn of which I was unaware.

As a private label vendor to True Value, I knew that we were vulnerable to being replaced. However, we were responsible for far more than providing the quality and delivery of Servess brand hand tools. We also maintained quality control and scheduled ocean freight shipments to five national distribution centers. In our own warehouse, we maintained high levels of Servess inventory so that we were never out of stock on the items customers relied upon.

In addition, Bernie Zurn and Dan Cotter expected us to create new products, promotions, updated packaging, and free displays.

We attended two True Value shows per year, at which we sold the Servess brand of tools to new True Value members. We provided special discounts for their monthly and seasonal promotions. Everyone was happy with the job we were doing, and they said so. We were confident in our future with True Value Hardware.

After several days visiting other factories in Korea, Bernie and I flew home on separate flights.

Although I spent a total of five days in close contact with Mr. Zurn, I did not feel that our relationship had improved. In fact, I found him to be detached and not willing to discuss future. I was forced into introducing him to the factories that were producing tools for his company. I had no choice.

I put aside my suspicions and the orders continued coming in as before. I put aside any fear that there was an ulterior motive in Mr. Zurn's request to travel to Korea on an inspection tour of his vendor's factories.

Over the course of the following months, my personal relationship with Mr. Zurn seemed to deteriorate. He was always anxious to end our conversations.

In 1984, the original Apple Macintosh personal computer (PC) first went on sale in January. The Macintosh cost about $2,500.00, but it sold well despite its high price. This was due in part to an iconic TV ad that ran during the 1984 Super Bowl. The ad is recognized as the greatest TV commercial ever created.

Trouble in River City (Chicago)

Every year, True Value holds two markets, one in Chicago and another in Memphis. We had a booth in both markets ever since we started doing business with them.

The dealer market in Memphis would take place in October 1984 at a large convention center.

The commitment to attend had to be received by the end of July 1984. We filled out the forms and included our check well in advance. A week later, I received a form letter from Cotter and Company. Our deposit check was returned. The letter said that all booths had been taken and so our company could not be accommodated.

We called the buyer, Bernie Zurn, and he said there was nothing he could do about it. However, Servess products would be displayed and sold at their own True Value display booth. After all, it was the company's private brand.

This represented an entirely new set of potentially fatal problems.

1. Without a display booth, we could not sell our own Omega precision tools to True Value dealers.

2. For the first time, there was a change in what had been a very cordial relationship with True Value.

3. Our agent in Korea reported that True Value had been in direct negotiations with the factory we had recently visited in Korea.

4. In addition, two additional factories that produced Servess tools for Omega had been contact by Mr. Zurn.

Normally in December, we would receive a pro forma purchase from True Value estimating requirements for the first six months of the following year. With this information, our factories would deliver our purchase orders on time, in full, as required by our customer.

When their new projected requirements did not arrive, I again called Mr. Zurn to remind him. He said that this year, there would be no advance schedule provided. I would have to make my own assumptions for the future.

The year 1984 ended with total sales of three million dollars, which was also the best year in the history of Omega.

Within two weeks, it became apparent that Cotter and Company, as the parent company of True Value Hardware Stores, had decided that as the volume, distribution, and quality of Servess products had proven profitable and successful for their members, going forward, they could manage it on their own without Omega.

Henceforth, they would place their own purchase orders with the same factories as before for direct delivery to each of their distribution centers. Eliminating Omega would lower their cost by 20 percent or more.

I soon received a letter thanking me for my support.

As a result, 1984 was the final year that Omega did business with True Value Hardware.

Chapter 37
Survival

The question at that moment was whether Omega would survive. More than forty-five employees might lose their jobs. However, interest rates on our bank loans were now close to 20 percent and we didn't have the cash flow to pay them down. The bank refused to extend our loans when they realized our key customer, True Value Hardware, had decided to buy direct from our sources and was dropping us their exclusive True Value (Servess brand) supplier of hand tools.

We had made the classic mistake of relying on a major national retail chain for more than 50 percent of our volume. It was a "deal with the devil." If you refused the opportunity of private brand, you would lose the account entirely. We agreed, and our volume soared, as well as our reputation for quality. For TrueValue, we were a Trojan horse. Once we had developed good quality products to produce under their company brand, they could buy direct from our proven factories at the same or perhaps lower prices than we could. That left us high and very dry.

Although I owed the bank for unpaid loans, there was more than enough in accounts receivable to cover the debt.

It took a while, but the bank and my creditors were paid. I had collected more than was owed and the difference belonged to me. It was badly needed.

True Value purchased our remaining inventory of Servess brand tools at their regular price. I then negotiated the sale of Omega Precision Hand Tools Inc. to

Royal Tools. The deal included a two-year employment contract for me as president of Omega Tools, a division of Royal Tools.

The forced sale of a business built from scratch is traumatic. It's as if you are driving straight along the highway at the speed limit with nothing up ahead when suddenly a big truck hits you from behind and forces you into a ditch.

We did not control the timing, although I should have known that sooner or later, the management of True Value would conclude that they no longer needed Omega. We had served our purpose and now it was over.

Note: Although their "factory door" cost was lowered by 20 percent, they still had to pay a trading company to oversee and consolidate the production of several factories in different cities and several countries.

A broker was necessary to "clear" containers at the port of entry. They could do all the above. What they could not do was to create new promotions, packaging, displays, and merchandising.

A wholesale distributor has an important role in the economy. The most successful have the capacity to purchase the best merchandise at favorable prices and to store, resell, and deliver at the lowest price to their customers.

Creating innovative products is the province of creative individuals. It is not the result of teamwork.

After three years of importing the same items from our former factories, Servess brand hand tools had nothing new to offer and sales fell off. After two years, Servess as a True Value brand was discontinued.

Although we had other customers who wanted to continue buying Omega tools, the reduced volume would not cover our overhead. Had Omega continued as a privately held company, it would have incurred ever larger losses. Royal Tools Inc. was anxious to buying Omega and we quickly came to a satisfactory price for the company. In addition, I would remain President of Omega, now a division of Royal Tools.

Working for a salary at Royal was extremely depressing. Although selling Omega had been the right thing to do, I wanted out. The problem was I had no idea what to do, and limited capital to invest.

In addition, I worried that at the age of fifty, I might be too old to start another business.

When my two-year employment contract with Royal ended, I decided to spend some time playing golf, taking life easy, and trying to figure out what I would do next. To outsiders, I had retired. In fact, I was unemployed.

Award Tool Company and Omega Tool Company had both been successful ventures, but they were in my past. Our son David was twenty-six. Susan, at twenty-two, had started law school.

Through the events of the 1980s, my marriage had remained strong. We were in the same house with two cars in the garage. Plus, the mortgage was finally paid off, I had some money in the bank, and no debt.

The bad news was I had no source of income and no prospects.

Chapter 38
Heart trouble

Suddenly, while driving, I felt my heart was beating too fast and irregularly. I drove to the office of my doctor, Larry Janoff. (I could just walk in, and he would see me as we were friends).

Larry did a cardiogram. It wasn't quite normal. For a long time, he had been following me for a heart murmur, but now he decided I needed to be seen by a cardiologist.

The cardiologist checked me out and although he agreed I had a heart murmur (this is where blood does not fully clear the arctic valve), there was no immediate emergency. I should wait.

I was telling this story to my friend Ronald Mandler and Ronald said I should go to St. Francis to be checked by another doctor. St. Francis Hospital is the best place for heart problems. I agreed and made an appointment to see a specialist.

The new doctor said an angiogram was the only way to know for sure what was going on and he ordered the test for the next day.

At the end of a long day, the results were finally in. The doctor said I had a very badly obstructed aortic valve, up to 90 percent closed due to calcification. It seems I have a bivalve (two leaves), not the usual Mercedes valve (three leaves). That caused the murmur that Doctor Larry heard so clearly.

I would need immediate surgery to replace the natural valve with a pig valve.

The next day, I underwent six hours of open heart sugary to replace the failing aortic valve with a new pig valve. The surgeon was Dr. Wisoff. This would be among the last open-heart surgeries he would perform after a very long and successful career at St. Francis.

Many friends visited me during that first heart surgery, among them were Carole and Steve Gutman, Carol and Donald Aronson, and Kenny and Roberta Lonoff.

My mother and father came to visit, but it was very brief. Before leaving, my mother told me she would not return because St. Francis is a Catholic hospital with symbols of "Christ on the cross" in every room. That was fine with me.

Chapter 39
A Bedroom Business

A friend of my son David called me to find out if I knew of any Asian factories that produced latex disposable gloves for export. Her company sold medical products and their supplier in Maylasia was unable to fill their orders as the demand for natural latex exceeded the supply.

I asked why latex gloves were suddenly in such demand. Her reply was that since the AIDS epidemic began two years earlier, latex gloves were the first line of defense to protect physicians and other health workers from this deadly disease. I kept this conversation in the back of my mind.

I told her my sources were in the hand tool industry and I could not help her.

Not long after that call, Pat was driving along Glen Cove Road and noticed a small store in a strip mall that sold women's sweaters. She turned into the parking area and went into the sweater store.

None of the sweaters appealed to her, but through an open door, Pat saw a large pegboard displaying an assortment of hand tools like those sold by Fuller Tool Company. Pat entered the room.

Two men were sitting at a table. The phones were ringing, and the fax machine was churning. If this was a tool sales operation, they sure were selling a lot of tools.

Pat asked one of the men if he knew her husband Buzz Fuller from the tool business. Yes, he knew me as I had done business with him over the years.

His name was Bob Klein. For many years, Bob Klein had been in the "closeout" business.

Bob and I had known each other since my days at Fuller Tool Company. He also knew that I had recently owned Omega Tools.

The phones never stopped. Bob explained that medical product buyers were calling to place orders for "container loads" of latex medical gloves under irrevocable letters of credit.

(Note: A letter of credit guarantees the exporting glove factory that the invoice will be paid when the merchandise is loaded aboard a ship and documented by a bill of lading. Additional factors may be stipulated on the letter of credit such as shipment on time, the quantity, quality, and price of the merchandise, and so on.)

A bank will issue a letter of credit to an importer with good credit.

During the entire time Pat was talking to Bob, the fax machine was printing out purchase orders for full containers (200,000 disposable gloves) along with the required letters of credit. When Pat got home, she told me what she had just witnessed.

The following day, I went to see Bob Klein in his office in the back of the sweater shop in Glen Cove. Since David's friend had asked about latex gloves, I wanted to find out what all the excitement was about. It could be an opportunity, but I needed to know more. Bob Klein would fill me in.

The story he told was this.

Before 1989, disposable gloves (latex and vinyl) were a minor medical supply item made and sold for physicians and surgeons. Gloves were not required for most dental procedures except during dental surgery.

In 1989, in response to the AIDS epidemic, the FDA required doctors, dentists, and other medical workers to wear disposable gloves as a barrier against this and other diseases. A huge demand for latex gloves suddenly occurred. Factories with little or no experience were exporting latex gloves, many of dubious quality.

The entire US supply was quickly depleted. It could take a year or more to fill the medical pipeline and to assure a steady supply of disposable gloves to every hospital, medical, and dental facility in the United States.

Latex is produced by the so-called rubber tree in tropical climates such as Thailand, Malaysia, and Indonesia. Rubber tire manufacturers had been the primary users, but now it was the medical profession at all levels. Clinics and hospitals quickly exhausted the US inventory of latex gloves. There was not enough raw latex to meet the overwhelming and sudden demand. Every day saw an increase in the price, only the highest bidder with a valid bank letter of credit could expect to receive delivery.

Before the demand for latex gloves exploded, a case of 1,000 gloves from Malaysia cost just fifteen dollars in the United States. At its peak, the cost per case reached ninety dollars.

The major American pharmaceutical companies, such as Johnson and Johnson, Baxter Medical, and a few others, were buying all the latex gloves they could find at whatever price was demanded. Hospitals, medical wholesalers, and physicians required an uninterrupted supply.

Bob Klein gave me a few samples of latex gloves. They were easy to get on and felt like a second skin. I held my hand under running water and, when the gloves were removed, my hands were dry.

It occurred to me that disposable gloves could be sold as inexpensive work gloves. The age-old question of "what if" popped into my head. What if ten latex gloves were packaged together and sold to consumers? Even at the current cost of ninety dollars per thousand (nine cents each), ten latex gloves could sell for less than the price of a pair of cotton gloves.

The next day, I went to back to the sweater shop on Glen Cove Road. I wanted more samples and to "blue sky" my idea with Bob Klein.

Bob thought the concept of latex gloves for consumers had merit. However, at that time, he was concerned with getting enough product to meet the demand from the medical profession. He thought it would be a long time before the supply of gloves would make my idea feasible.

Bob graciously gave me a box of one hundred gloves and asked that I let him know if I decided to proceed.

I needed to try latex disposable gloves for household chores and began experimenting. I used a pair to paint a railing and to clean leaves from a clogged gutter. I used them to change the oil in my car.

The possible uses for low-cost disposable gloves seemed endless.

Work gloves are sold in the same hardware stores as hand tools. In most companies, the tool buyer and the glove buyer is the same person. I knew all the hardware and paint distributors, national hardware Co-ops, Discount stores, and big box retail chains.

My concept all came down to one this simple question. Would consumers prefer one pair of cotton gloves for $1.29 or ten disposable gloves for ninety-nine cents? That was the question.

I needed to discuss the idea with someone whose opinion I valued. I called Marty Katz. Marty had been in the hardware business for as many years as I had. He had been a sale rep for Great Neck Saw, Royal Tools, and others. Marty would give me an honest appraisal. If he didn't think it was a good idea, I probably would have found someone who would agree with me.

Marty loved the idea. He told me that if I went ahead and formed a new company to package and market low-cost disposable gloves for consumers, he would be glad to represent my company. That was what I wanted to hear.

Chapter 40
Fish or Cut Bait!

Hand Care Inc. was established in December 1989 under the laws of New York state. Harrison Fuller was the president and Pat Fuller was Secretary. Our lawyer was Marty's sister. The price was right.

Since my earliest days at Fuller Tool Company, I believed that the path to successful sales and distribution of a generic product was superior packaging.

My first business, Award Tools Inc., was created specifically for a new retail environment: the discount store. Award Tools had succeeded beyond everyone's expectation.

My second business venture, Omega Precision Hand Tools Inc. quickly become recognized as a high-quality line of precision tools for hobbyists and ordinary consumers.

Now at fifty-five years of age, I would start my third and last business.

We had a name for the new business and a business plan. We did not have a source for disposable gloves.

My dentist suggested that I ask his supplier, Baxter Medical, as they had supplied him with latex gloves. They might have latex gloves that failed to meet the quality Baxter required. If so, they would likely be available at a very reduced or even a closeout price. It sounded like a good idea.

I called Baxter Medical and asked if they had any closeout gloves available. They said I should call Mr. Jim Stigleman and gave me his phone number.

Jim told me that he had been a production manager for Baxter but had recently resigned to start his own company, Innovative Enterprise Ltd. Jim had an exclusive contract with Baxter Medical to purchase all latex and vinyl exam gloves that did not meet FDA standards for medical use.

Under the agreement, Jim guaranteed Baxter that the rejected gloves would not be sold for any medical purpose. They could be sold as general-purpose gloves and clearly labeled "not for medical use."

During our conversation, Jim disclosed that there was very little demand for non-medical disposable gloves. He was having difficulty finding customers.

I proposed a solution that would meet the terms of his contract with Baxter Medical.

My new company, Hand Care Inc., would purchase and repackage his gloves for resale as Hand Care disposable gloves for painting, gardening, cleaning, and so on. Every Hand Care repackage would be clearly labeled "Not for Medical Use."

We would have an unlimited supply of gloves from an American supplier purchased for pennies on the dollar. It was a winning solution for Jim and for our nascent business.

I could not take delivery of gloves until securing a place to store them. I contacted ACRMD in Jamaica in Queens, about twenty minutes away. ACRMD is a state-supported workshop and training facility for autistic and/or handicapped young adults.

ACRMD agreed to take delivery of our gloves, and the material for packaging and shipping. They could assemble our gloves into a variety of finished products, fill our customers' orders, and have them ready for delivery by UPS or truck. ACRMD would bill Hand Care at a fixed price for each individual item they shipped, no contract required.

Our first one hundred cases of general-purpose disposable gloves were soon shipped from Innovative Enterprise in Indiana to our fulfillment facility in Jamaica, Queens, New York.

Miles Godin (Burton-Miles ad agency) designed the polybag and the artwork for our first two items.

Star Polybag Company delivered 10,000 Hand Care ten-piece polybags. General Box Company delivered 1,000 Hand Care one hundred-piece boxes.

ACRMD took delivery of gloves, polybags, and dispenser boxes. It had been only three months since Pat had stopped in the sweater store on Glen Cove Road.

We were ready to ship. All we needed were customers.

Marty Katz had lined up his cadre of sales agents. Every sales rep was supplied with as many ten-piece polybags and dispenser boxes as needed to give away to their potential customers. I wanted every buyer to personally experience the quality and value of our disposable work gloves, just as I had.

It wasn't long before we got our first order. Soon, it was off to the races!

Before our first year ended, our line of disposable gloves had grown to include a polybag of six gloves, a dispenser box of fifty gloves, plus our most popular item, a the twenty-five-piece "Bag O' Gloves."

Marty and his team of sales agents were getting orders from hardware and paint distributors, supermarket chains, drug store chains, and food service companies

Our First Hand Care Product

Our First Item #108

About two years after Hand Care Inc. introduced disposable gloves to American consumers as a low-cost alternative to expensive work gloves, I received a call from a friend in Los Angeles. I had met Gary Tobias years before, when he was a sales manager of a company that made several items for Omega Tools.

Gary was now sales manager of a medical products company that sold medical latex gloves to Lowe's Home Centers across the United States. His buyer was looking for a less expensive line of disposable gloves, which Gary's medical products company could not provide.

She asked my friend if he knew anything about Hand Care disposable gloves for consumers. The glove buyer for Lowe's had seen our Hand Care disposable gloves in her local ACE hardware store.

Susan Smith told me that her father used latex gloves for years for painting, cleaning, and working on his boat.

Fortunately, Gary Tobias had my name and phone number and gave them to the Lowe's buyer. Susan called me soon after.

Although Lowe's corporate offices were in Wilmington, North Carolina, I quickly arranged to fly down for a meeting. Susan met me in the reception area and escorted me to her office.

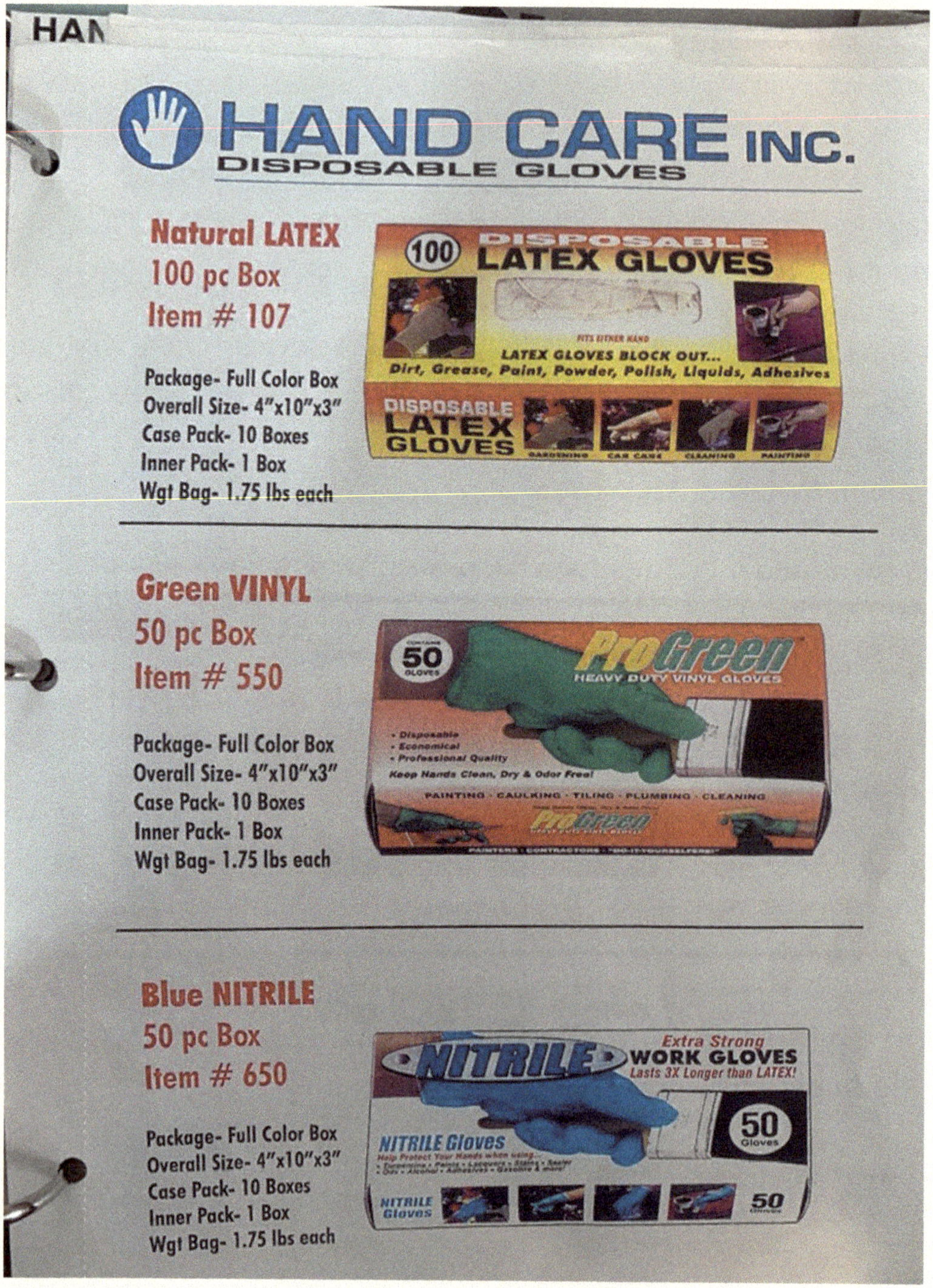

HAND CARE INC.
DISPOSABLE GLOVES

Natural LATEX
100 pc Box
Item # 107

Package- Full Color Box
Overall Size- 4"x10"x3"
Case Pack- 10 Boxes
Inner Pack- 1 Box
Wgt Bag- 1.75 lbs each

Green VINYL
50 pc Box
Item # 550

Package- Full Color Box
Overall Size- 4"x10"x3"
Case Pack- 10 Boxes
Inner Pack- 1 Box
Wgt Bag- 1.75 lbs each

Blue NITRILE
50 pc Box
Item # 650

Package- Full Color Box
Overall Size- 4"x10"x3"
Case Pack- 10 Boxes
Inner Pack- 1 Box
Wgt Bag- 1.75 lbs each

The local ACE hardware store had told her that Hand Care brand disposable gloves were his best-selling line of work gloves, especially the twenty-five piece "Bag O' Gloves."

Clearly, the Lowes buyer had already decided to stock Hand Care gloves at Lowe's Home Centers even before I got there. The most important question she had for me was whether Hand Care had the capacity to supply Lowe's orders completely and quickly. I assured her that we did.

I left her office with an official Lowe's purchase order for 25,000 ten-piece packages of latex gloves, 25,000 Bags O' Gloves, and 5,000 dispenser boxes. This was for only 200 eastern district stores. Once they had a history of the rate of sales in their eastern stores, they would add the line to 1,800 Lowe's stores across the United States.

We had thirty days to ship, or their computer would automatically cancel the order. Needless to say, it was "all hands-on deck." We shipped the complete order in less than ten days.

A funny thing happens when your line is seen in a high-profile retail chain. We were getting calls from companies we didn't know but who had seen our product at Lowe's. Hand Care Inc. suddenly had national credibility in the glove market.

Chapter 41
The Home Depot

"Little White Lies"

I had tried countless times to contact the northeast division buyer for Home Depot and never was able to get through. I was talking to a recorded voice and my calls were not returned. I learned from others that this was commonplace. A vendor could not simply call Home Depot and expect to get an appointment to show his or her products.

The Home Depot sold more paint and paint supplies than anyone else in the country. Our various packages of low-cost disposable gloves would sell very fast in their paint department.

Every year, The Home Depot conducts an event called the Line Review. During this event, every item is evaluated, and new items are presented. The Line Review is limited to current vendors and a few prospective vendors. Without an invitation to the Review, there is no acceptable pathway to becoming a vendor to The Home Depot. As a new company, Hand Care would not be invited to the annual Line Review. There had to be another way.

During a vacation in Florida in March 1992, my plan was conceived.

This is a true story, which I hope comes to the attention of The Home Depot. It is a lesson on why a successful consumer goods company should encourage creative thinkers. Big companies should keep an open mind (and doors) and encourage innovation. Building barriers to innovation is not progress.

In March 1992, Pat and I were at our new vacation home in Florida. Bernie Marcus, a founder of The Home Depot, and his wife lived nearby in the same community. Our friend Roberta Lonoff and Mrs Marcus were good friends and often played golf together.

Robera and Kenny Lonoff had recently been invited to a dinner party at the Marcus home. I imagined what I would say to Bernie Marcus had Pat and I been invited to that dinner party.

It is likely I would have mentioned that my company made disposable gloves but I had not been able to get an appointment with his buyer in New Jersey. In my imagination, Mr Marcus would agree that Hand Care gloves should be in every Home Depot store and that I should write a letter to the head of the NorthEast Division about our conversation.

On returning to my office, I composed the letter that the imaginary Bernie Marcus had suggested. The letter described my imaginary conversation with Bernie Marcus at the imaginary dinner party. My letter said we were friends of the Marcus family and members of the same golf club in Florida.

During my imaginary conversation, I told Bernie I owned a glove company that made disposable gloves for painting, cleaning, and home maintenance. I said that Bernie believed disposable gloves would be a good product line for The Home Depot and that I should contact the president of the NorthEast Division. The letter made it appear as if the dinner party and the conversation had actually happend.

I had no qualms about creating a false narrative and was confident that no one would call Mr. Marcus to validate my letter. Even if someone did, I was not getting anywhere and felt the risk was worth it.

I mailed the letter on a Monday. At 9:00 a.m. on Wednesday morning, the paint buyer for the Home Depot NorthEast Division called. He wanted to know if I could be at his office at 11:00 a.m. the next day with samples of Hand Care disposable gloves. I said I would rearrange my schedule to accommodate his request.

HAND CARE INC.
DISPOSABLE GLOVES
P.O. Box 331 · Albertson, New York 11507 TEL: 516-747-5649 FAX: 516-747-2077

ASSORTMENT #1009
Contains the Top Selling Disposable Work Gloves!
(Delivered in 1 Carton)

GOOD

108 10pc Natural LATEX-Bag
(12 Bags in Assmt. #1009)
Open Stock: 12 w/Clip Strip

725 25 pc LATEX-Bag
(6 Bags in Assmt. #1009)
Open Stock: 12 w/Clip Strip

107 100 pc LATEX-Box
(3 Boxes in Assmt. #1009)
Open Stock: Min. 1 Box

BETTER

506 6pc Heavy VINYL-Tag
(12 Tags in Assmt. #1009)
Open Stock: 12 w/Clip Strip

515 15pc Heavy VINYL-Bag
(6 Bags in Assmt. #1009)
Open Stock: 12 w/Clip Strip

550 50pc Heavy VINYL-Box
(3 Boxes in Assmt. #1009)
Open Stock: Min. 1 Box

BEST

606 6pc NITRILE-Tag
(12 Tags in Assmt. #1009)
Open Stock: 12 w/Clip Strip

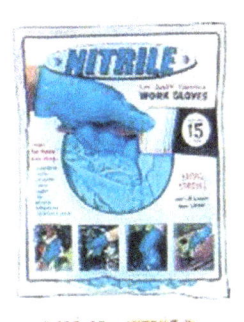

615 15pc NITRILE-Bag
(6 Bags in Assmt. #1009)
Open Stock: 12 w/Clip Strip

650 50pc NITRILE-Box
(3 Boxes in Assmt. #1009)
Open Stock: Min. 1 Box

HAND CARE Inc.
BioDegradable LATEX Gloves

PO BOX 331
Toll Free 800 494 7590
FAX 1 516 747 2077

ALBERTSON NY 11507
Email: hfuller@optonline.net

Latex Gloves

100pc Box #107

24pc Bag #225

10pc Bag #108

50pc Box #150

Go Green!

- *Latex is a 'Renewable Resource'*
- *Latex Gloves are BioDegradable!*
- *Vinyl & Nitrile Gloves are __NOT__!*

The next day at 11:00 a.m., I was in his office.

The weight of Mr. Marcus's suggestion was working. Within the hour, a computer had printed an opening purchase order to Hand Care for 900 Home Depot stores. The order included our three best-selling packages: ten-piece latex gloves, the twenty-five piece Bag O Gloves, and a dispenser box of 100 latex gloves. Hand Care gloves would be in every Home Depot from Maine to Pittsburgh and south to Richmond, Virginia.

Over the next ten years, the original three SKUs grew to twelve SKUs and our annual sales to The Home Depot would exceed two million dollars.

Lowe's was the first national retailer to carry Hand Care gloves, followed by The Home Depot and Menards plus wholesale distributors and retailers. We were growing exponentially.

Auto mechanics, homeowners, do-it-yourselfers, commercial users, contractors, and countless others began buying low-cost, disposable gloves for the first time. They would return for more again and again.

Jim Stigleman had been supplying Baxter gloves at good prices, but it could not last. As a child, Jim had contracted polio and although he had recovered, the disease was only dormant. Gradually, Jim began to show signs that it had returned, and it soon disabled him.

Jim passed away shortly after the recurrence. Jim was a Vietnam veteran and a wonderful person. He was honest as the Indiana farm boy he was with a keen mind and a dry sense of humor. I was very sad to learn of his untimely passing.

Innovative Enterprises was sold to The Safety Zone and our dependable supply of low-cost gloves from a domestic supplier was in jeopardy. We had just three months of inventory and had to act fast.

"As one door closes, another opens." My former agent for Omega Tools in the Far East came to the rescue. By then, the supply of latex gloves from Malaysia had caught up to the demand and prices had stabilized from the unreasonable levels of just a few years before.

Several glove factories were now anxious to fill Hand Care's glove requirements. One factory offered to package Hand Care gloves in polybags and dispenser boxes produced and printed in Malaysia using our artwork and to our specifications.

This meant that we could import full containers of our most popular items directly to the ACRMD warehouse in Jamaica at a lower cost than ever before.

With great anticipation, I waited for our initial delivery of finished product from our new source in Malaysia. I needn't have worried.

Our former agent for hand tools had successfully found a very reliable factory to supply for our growing sales of latex and nitrile disposable gloves.

Special gloves, such as heavy-duty green vinyl, would continue to be sourced locally and packaged at ACRMD.

Customers would order different gloves in various quantities and sizes. Assembling complicated orders, ready to pack and ship, required close supervision by management.

Years before, for a True Value promotion, Omega Tools had delivered a full container of fourteen-inch pipe wrenches direct from Spain to Chicago. It was for a nationwide sale called "Tool of the Month."

We had successfully shipped the merchandise from our overseas factory to their warehouse in Chicago at considerable savings to meet the special promotion sale price True Value required.

I decided to propose a similar promotion for The Home Depot. Hand Care would deliver a full container (20,000 dispenser boxes) of disposable gloves direct to their distribution center in New Jersey at a discount of 25 percent.

The Home Depot would advertise our 100-piece dispener box in every local newspaper at 25 percent below the regular retail price.

The container was delivered on time and every Home Depot store was completely sold out. They would repeat this and other direct to warehouse promotions at least once every year.

Hand Care disposable gloves quickly became the best selling product line (except for paint) in the paint department of every Home Depot store.

Chapter 42
A Musical Recital

One of my fondest memories of my youth was hearing and seeing Isaac Stern perform up close and personal at a recital in the living room of my friend Joel Gitlin.

In 1999, I invited a young and talented violinist to perform in the living room of our home in Roslyn. About twenty-five friends were there to see and hear Anton Polezhayev up close. Anton was accompanied on our Steinway piano by his mother Elena.

After performing a repertoire of classical violin selections, Anton exchanged his professional instrument for the student violin I had learned to play many years earlier. The difference in the sound was immediately obvious. We all had a good laugh.

It was a wonderful recital and fulfilled a wish that had long been on my bucket list.

However, that was not the end of the story of my student violin.

After the concert, Anton asked if he could borrow it for his younger brother who had just started violin lessons but did not have his own instrument. I readily agreed. Since then, my violin has been loaned to a high school student who played in her school orchestra. Currently, it is at a music school in Manhasset owned by a classically trained violinist, Roslyn Huang. The instrument I had from age eleven has become another "red violin," destined to be used by other young music students.

Chapter 43
A Remarkable Coincidence

It was becoming obvious that my parents, Bernie and Helen Fuller, could no longer maintain their apartment on Singer Island. They had lived there for the past fifteen years or more. Now it was not clean, there was little food in the fridge, and all their friends had long since passed away. They were isolated.

They moved into a kosher assisted living facility in Boca Raton, closer to my sister June. My older sister Dee lived in Fort Lauderdale, thirty minutes away.

My parents now had a personal aide. The one-bedroom apartment was bright and nicely furnished. When I visited them, they seemed quite content in their new surroundings.

One afternoon, Bernie Fuller got into a conversation with a widower by the name of Louis Weiner. They began trading stories about their children and grandchildren.

They had a lot in common as both had grandchildren living in Israel. There were other coincidences. All their grandchildren had been raised in the United States. Both of their oldest grandsons were studying to become rabbis. Their wives were both daughters of "survivors." Eventually, Bernie Fuller and Louis Wiener realized they were talking about the same family in Israel.

After Dee and Jerry Hahn were divorced, Jerry married Lynn Weiner (Louis Weiner's daughter). Lynn became the stepmother to Jonathon Hahn and grandmother to the many children born in Israel.

Lynn frequenty visited the ever-expanding family in Israel and was (and is) loved by her many step-grandchildren and great grandchildren. I am told there are more than fifty Hahn family descendants living in Israel as of this writing.

Not long after this unusual encounter, Louis Weiner passed away.

Chapter 44
Bad Vibes

I got a call from my younger sister June. This was unusual.

She told me that our father had an intestinal blockage that was causing him problems. The doctor said they could resolve the blockage with medication, but to rule out cancer, he would perform an investigative colonoscopy.

Having suffered for years with ulcerative colitis, I had more than a few colonoscopies myself. I knew how difficult they were to prepare for and that there were risks for older people.

Even if they found evidence of cancer, for a ninety-one-year-old patient, there was little anyone could do. The patient could not undergo chemotherapy. I felt it would be wiser to first resolve the blockage that was causing discomfort.

The fact was they were going to operate on my father.

I asked June for the name of the doctor. June gave me his name.

I called his doctor to discuss the situation, to make my case, and to listen to his reasoning. He refused to speak to me.

I told his nurse to give him the following message: "If he operates on my ninety-one-year-old father and serious medical complications or death resulted, I will sue him for malpractice."

That same afternoon, I flew to Miami, rented a car, and went immediately to the hospital. I had intended to discuss the problem with his doctor before anyone operated on him.

However, by the time I got there, he had already had the colonoscopy and was resting in his room, although still under the effect of sedation. We had a nice talk.

The next morning, I phoned my mother, who was at their apartment on Belle Isle Miami Beach. I offered to pick her up and take her to the hospital with me that morning.

When I arrived at her building, she was waiting for me out front. Without returning my greeting (a kiss on the cheek), she got in my rental car and proceeded to scream at me all the way to the hospital.

Her anger had nothing to do with my father's health or anything at all to do with my father. She was upset that upon landing in Miami I did not call her before going to the hospital. Also, I did not take her to dinner the night before. As usual, I shut up. I dropped her off at the hospital entrance and proceeded to park my car in the hospital parking lot some distance away.

By the time I arrived at the large private room on the exclusive sixth floor (reserved for *big* donors to the hospital), both of my sisters, Dee and June, and my mother, were already there.

Again, I got no greeting from anyone. (Oh, yes, Dad said hello.)

There was no conversation regarding my father's condition. He was fine. All three of them accused me of wanting my father to die. That was the reason I tried to stop the colonoscopy. It was very clear.

Of course, I protested that I was only trying to protect him and that a second opinion should have been sought. He was lucky it had worked out, but it might not have.

My father said nothing, even when I asked him if he believed I wanted him to die (and leave me his money). He refused to answer.

Suddenly, Dee reached for a phone and asked for security to be sent up to the room as "someone" was causing a disturbance.

Within thirty seconds, a very tall Florida trooper, complete with a sidearm, appeared at the door. My sister pointed to me and said, "Remove that man." The trooper asked me to follow him, which I did. He then asked if I had my own transportation. If not, he would call for a police vehicle to take me to police headquarters, where I could get a cab.

Horrified at being accused of wanting my own father dead, and everything that had recently transpired, I drove forty-five miles to Palm Beach airport in thirty minutes, turned in my Hertz car, and caught the first available flight home.

As upset as I was, I knew that as long as one or both parents were alive, I would eventually see my sisters again. At that point in time, it was the last thing I could possibly want.

CHAPTER 45
Their Final Act

My mother's emphysema had gotten so bad that she breathed with the aid of an oxygen tank. One time, she was taken by ambulance to the hospital.

Although her problem was not too serious and was quickly remedied, Bernie thought that she would not be coming back ever again.

Apparently, he did not wish to live alone and died in his sleep that same night. Helen came home the next day, but Bernie was already gone.

My sister June called me at home and gave me the news. However, she failed to mention when and where the funeral service was to be held. I made a call to Lynn Hahn and got the information. Pat had pneumonia at the time and couldn't go. David went in her place.

About fifty people gathered in the chapel of the cemetery. David and I didn't know the assembled mourners as they were either friends of Dee or June.

At a Jewish funeral, it is necessary for a family member to identify the body. This fell to me.

I made my speech, which included some defining stories about our relationship that were either funny or illustrative. Naturally, it was very complimentary. I lauded his success in business, his work on behalf of Israel, and a few other things. Few of those assembled had any idea of our tortured relationship and this was not the place to enlighten them.

The evening of the funeral, David and I sat *shiva* at June's apartment. It was in a luxury apartment building on the property of the Boca Raton Hotel. We were surprised to learn that sister Deborah occupied the adjoining apartment, and that it was the same size (very large) as the one we were in. The next morning, David and I flew home.

Naturally, I was more than curious regarding any inheritance that my father may have left. It wasn't long before I found out.

June called a week or so later and told me that Dad had left me a sum of money. All I had to do was sign some papers and the check would be on its way. I will not disclose the amount, but it was more than I expected under the circumstances.

I asked what the will said with respect to the balance of his estate and June told me that she and Deborah were the sole inheritors of the balance of his estate, from which they would support our mother for the rest of her life (Mother was ninety-four years old at that point).

In their older age, when they were past ninety, our parents turned all their financial and legal responsibilities over to their younger daughter, June, and to a lesser degree, to Dee. This included management of their daily bills such as rent, utilities, insurance, and so on. June, in turn, authorized their local bank to pay these recurring bills through auto pay.

The Bernard and Helen Fuller Foundation was turned over to the daughters. It soon closed.

Hand Care Inc. immediately sent one hundred cases of latex gloves to those working to recover the dead and attend to the wounded. The trucking company that delivered the gloves to the "pile," as the site was called, also donated their service.

Chapter 46
Growing Pains

By then, it was clear that ACRMD was too small and too slow to satisfy the daily requirements of national accounts such as Lowe's and The Home Depot. Our home office fax machine would ring twenty-four hours a day with orders that had to be filled immediately. Something had to be done to increase our shipping capacity.

The alternative, which I refused to seriously consider, was to rent our own warehouse, purchase steel racks, fill them with inventory, and hire twenty or more workers for packaging, product assembly, and shipping plus a qualified full-time bookkeeper.

The (old-fashioned) "all in-house" operation that I knew from Fuller Tool Company, Award Tool Company, and Omega Tools was out. Computers, email, and fax machines had replaced secretaries, communication by cable, and much more. I didn't want to pay for pensions, medical insurance, or workers' compensation.

I preferred to out-source as much as possible. Out-sourcing allows you to know the real cost of every product. We knew the cost of gloves, a polybag, and the labor to assemble. Each month, ACRMD billed for the total quantity of individual items assembled and shipped on our behalf. We did not pay for storage space.

A proprietary production facility has ongoing expenses, such as labor, rent, utilities, and so on even if sales are insufficient to cover them all. That was a trap I was unwilling to fall into.

By 2002, Hand Care was grossing three million dollars in annual sales. To fill very large orders from The Home Depot and Lowe's, we arranged for our prime vendor, The Safety Zone, to ship directly to them. Orders from smaller accounts, like Ace Hardware Stores, continued to be shipped from ACRMD in Jamaica, Queens.

The Safety Zone became our second and largest outsource facility. It worked very smoothly. Orders were shipped on time, with no mistakes. The product was of good quality. This kept the buyers at Lowe's and at The Home Depot very quiet, which meant they were "happy" with Hand Care as their supplier.

Billing, receivables, filing, sales, and marketing were all managed by me, my wife Pat, and Betty Edwards in the former bedrooms of our two children, David and Susan.

We outsourced everything from gloves to packaging and shipping supplies. ACRMD and The Safety Zone produced and delivered our customer orders on time and complete.

Lowe's Home Centers, Home Depot, ACE Hardware, and our other large national retailers did not know that Hand Care Disposable Gloves was a small business managed by me and my wife Pat, with Betty Edwards, from a bedroom at our home in Roslyn, New York.

On December 21, 2001, The Home Depot announced that a new chief executive had been appointed. His name was Bob Nardelli. Nardelli was know as "Chainsaw" Bob due to his infamous reputation as a slash and burn manager who primarily reduced payroll. One of his first decisions was to centralize all purchasing at corporate headquarters in Atlanta.

At the time, Home Depot operated nine divisions around the country. Each had its own buyers who selected the best and most appropriate products to carry in their market. Snow blowers were a major item in the northeast division. Beach chairs were sold all year in Florida.

The first thing Bob Nardelli did was to close every division buying office and centralize buying at the main office in Atlanta. Our buyer had been with Home Depot for twenty years and, at the age of forty-five, was immediately let go.

In a letter dated December 21, 2001, I was informed that The Home Depot would henceforth import their disposable gloves directly from our source in Malaysia. The letter thanked me for my service and wished me good luck.

The Home Depot was working from the same playbook as True Value Hardware had used sixteen years before.

The big difference now was that Hand Care could survive very easliy without The Home Depot.

We had no factory rent and employed no workers. Our only employee was Betty Edwards, who worked part time at home. We were still Lowe's exclusive supplier of disposable gloves and sold hundreds of hardware stores and paint distributors.

Chapter 47
Moving On

Before coming to Hand Care, Betty Edwards had been the manager of the Jamaica ACRMD workshop. Her job was filled by an inexperienced person, who did not have the skills to be a plant manager. As a result, we had fallen behind in our obligation to deliver customer orders in a timely manner. In addition, our inventory was not maintained as it was when Betty Edwards was the supervisor.

Bad as the ACRMC situation had become, it was still manageable. Eventually, a rumor began to circulate that ACRMD would not renew its lease and would relocate to a smaller facility.

They invited me to look over the new facility. It was impossible to park there, the loading dock served five other companies, and fifty-three-foot trailers could not fit into the single narrow loading dock.

The actual workspace consisted of multiple small rooms, which meant almost no supervision. It was a disaster in the making, over which I had no control.

A month later, our inventory was transferred to the new, smaller warehouse. From then on, things went from bad to worse.

The smaller production facility was unable keep up with our orders. I decided the time had come to sell Hand Care before it was too late.

The obvious buyer of Hand Care was The Safety Zone. They were already importing on our behalf and had been filling our Lowe's warehouse orders for a long time.

I broached the subject with Sandy Seidman, the owner of Safety Zone. He was interested in keeping the Lowe's business but had no interest in our hardware accounts. Although this was a very solid part of our business, it was outside of the core business of The Safety Zone.

Lowe's, however, was a very valuable account. The Safety Zone, on behalf of Hand Care, had been importing and filling our Lowe's orders for several years. Safety Zone wanted to continue shipping to Lowe's.

Sandy offered to buy the Lowe's account from Hand Care and to pay me a generous royalty for the next five years. The deal would include any new items that Lowe's might add from the extensive Safety Zone catalog. We had a deal.

To this day, The Safety Zone is still the main source of disposable gloves and other safety products for Lowe's. The original Hand Care polybags of ten and twenty-five gloves and the box of 100 disposable gloves remain the bestselling items.

At that point, we no longer had The Home Depot account and had spun off the Lowe's account. In addition, ACRMD was not doing a good job. The time had come to sell Hand Care Inc.

Akers Industries in Boston had been our backup supplier of gloves for more than ten years. Akers had often expressed interest in buying Hand Care Inc.

The sale was finalized in May of 2009. For the next five years, Akers sent me a (sizeable) royalty check for every order of Hand Care gloves they shipped. I could finally retire!

CHAPTER 48
Madoff and Me

This story is out of the time sequence (December 2008).

The Madoff scheme was the largest Ponzi scheme of all time. It affected many people who were close to me and other people who were part of the Jewish community in New York and Florida.

Richard Spring had been on top of the world. He used private jets, stayed at top hotels in New York, belonged to two country clubs, and owned house in Florida. Richard patronized the best restaurants and was an art collector. Bernie Madoff had made Richard Spring very rich—until he wasn't.

Pat first met Richard Spring when both families belonged to Glen Oaks Country Club in the 1950s. When Richard married Jeanne, the two women became very close friends.

Jeanne Spring was a beautiful woman with many talents, from golf to art to gardening and more. She also had a great sense of humor, so much so that whenever I heard Pat laughing while on the phone, I knew she was talking to Jeanne.

When Jeanne passed away from pancreatic cancer, Pat stayed in touch with Richard, at least for a while.

When the news of the Madoff Ponzi scheme broke in *The New York Times*, we were enjoying our morning coffee. The phone rang. It was our friend Steve Gutman.

Steve knew that Richard Spring, as a salesman for Madoff Securities, had convinced many friends, club members, and even relatives to invest with Madoff. Based on our friendship with the Spring family, Steve worried that we were victims of Bernie Madoff.

In fact, I asked Richard to get me into Madoff, but he said the amount was too small. However, his son Adam had recently joined a new "fund of funds" and needed clients.

Richard assured me that the fund of funds had money with Madoff and my account would grow right along with Madoff. Besides, I would be doing Richard and Adam a favor. I agreed.

My investment with Adam's firm was growing month after month. However, the monthly statement did not indicate what was bought and what was sold. It only stated the current value of my account. When I requested more information, they refused. I found their lack of transparency very disturbing. I told Adam I wanted out.

When Madoff confessed to running a Ponzi, the managers admitted that the Fund had invested 100% of their clients money with Madoff. There was nothing left.

For anyone who doesn't know, the Madoff investment scandal was a major case of stock and securities fraud. In December of 2008, a former NASDAQ chairman and founder of the Wall Street firm Bernard L. Madoff Investments LLC, admitted it was an elaborate Ponzi scheme.

Every media outlet in the country announced that the Madoff Fund was broke. It had all been a fraud—a fifty-billion-dollar Ponzi scheme.

Richard Spring, a salesman for Madoff, told *The Wall Street Journal* that he personally lost over eleven million dollars. In addition, he had invested the life savings of his three children and other family members in the Madoff fraud.

I was "saved" from a similar fate only because Richard urged me to invest with his son Adam. Adam needed the business and Richard assured me he would oversee my investments. "No need to worry," he said. Fortunately, I did worry.

Helen Fuller 1907–2002

Not long after our mother became a widow, June and Dee could see no reason for her to remain in assisted living. Since Bernie was gone, she didn't need such a large and expensive apartment.

They moved Helen, along with her aide, into a small, ground-floor, rundown apartment in a poor neighborhood.

On a trip to Florida to visit Jerry Hahn in the hospital, Pat and I visited the apartment. At the time, my mother, who was almost ninety-five years of age, was suffering from dementia and lung disease. I can only say that it was disgusting. The toilet didn't work. She slept in a hallway while the aide had the bedroom. The kitchen was dirty. The outside area was littered with garbage and small animals roamed freely.

Eventually, my sisters moved our mother into the aide's family apartment in North Fort Lauderdale. Helen was now a boarder in the aide's apartment.

Pat and I visited my mother while at the aide's apartment. She thought I was her brother Gilbert who had died many years before.

Helen Fuller passed away two months later. She was ninety-five years old.

Chapter 49
"Find a Need and Package It!

For me, the concept of "retirement" does not fit the customary definition of most of my peers. To them, "retirement" is six months in Florida, eighteen holes of golf, gin rummy, watching the stock market, afternoon naps, and drinks and dinner with friends. They are ROMEOs: Retired Old Men Eating Out.

In 2011, a couple of years after I "retired," I realized my creative juices were still dumping ideas into my brain. By then, however, I had no means of bringing my ideas to life.

I could, of course, have presented my ideas to Stu Perlmutter at Akers Industries, the new owner of Hand Care. Stu is a good businessman and had built a fine company, but he prefers the "tried and true."

Sandy Seidman had always been open to my ideas. As the sole owner of The Safety Zone, he ran a two hundred-million-dollar company with five distribution centers around the United States. Disposable gloves had become the best-selling products among thousands of other safety products.

Safety Zone had been very important to the success of Hand Care. During our fifteen year-long relationship, Sandy's company produced, filled, and shipped Hand Care purchase orders to Lowe's and The Home Depot.

I had always enjoyed a good personal relationship with Sandy. We would meet for long lunches or whenever I had a new marketing idea that I thought might benefit both of us.

In 2010, Sandy Seidman, a kid from Brooklyn, sold The Safety Zone for forty million dollars and retired to Florida and a big yacht.

Since 1967, when I was banished from the family business, my energy and creative ability was devoted to regaining the financial security that I had grown up with. My story is not about growing up poor and seeking financial security; it is about growing up in comfort, losing it, and striving to recover financial security.

Award Tools, Omega Tools, and Hand Care (disposable gloves) were all successful. I can't leave out Sandy Epstein, who invested my savings in good, long-term growth stocks.

CHAPTER 50
THE TRUTH WILL OUT!

Not to beat a "dead horse," but it defies religion, tradition, and normal behavior for a parent to dispose of a son as easily as dismissing a worker he claimed (without evidence) of stealing merchandise.

Miles Godin had long since replaced Frank Fox as the exclusive ad agency for Fuller Tool Co. and Fuller Tool was Miles's largest account by far.

Before my father passed away, he summoned Miles Godin to his office. Before he began, Miles was told that what he was about to learn was strictly confidential. If he told anyone before he (Bernie) passed away, the Burton-Miles ad agency would immediately and forever lose Fuller Tool Co as an account.

"Is that perfectly clear?"

Miles said he understood the consequences and said he would not tell anyone what he was about to learn, until after BHF was gone.

This is what my father told Miles.

> In June 1967, when Buzz was in India and in Cannes with Pat, Lillian, the company bookkeeper, told me that she had witnessed Buzz selling inventory from his car, that he had opened a "secret" bank account, and was "padding" his travel expenses.

When I confronted Buzz about it, he denied everything. He said he never sold merchandise from his car, there is no "secret" bank account, and his expense account was accurate.

I did not believe him as there was no reason for Lillian to lie as she had been a loyal employee for many years. However, I never investigated if her claims were true, although I should have.

Instead, I discussed the matter with my lawyer. Together, in Montreal, we devised a plan that we were sure Buzz would accept. However, it did not work out as we thought it would.

When I returned from Montreal, I told Buzz that he had been seen selling company merchandise from his car, for cash, and had been padding his travel expenses, plus other crimes. The consequences if he wants to remain with the company (and the family) are a demotion, with a cut in salary and some other things. [He could not recall what the "other things" were.]

Buzz denied everything and asked me where the stories came from and who was spreading lies about him. I said nothing.

What I am about to tell you must remain strictly between us.

However, after I am gone, you are free to tell Buzz everything.

Here we go!
These are his exact words, according to Miles.

A few years after Buzz left the company, I told Lillian that it was time for her to retire. She had been the company bookkeeper for nearly forty years.

Lillian became very upset and said that before she left, there was something I should know.

She told me that Buzz had never sold merchandise from his car, there was no secret bank account, and he never padded expenses. She said she made it all up because Buzz was going to fire her.

She knew I would believe her, and that I might fire Buzz instead.

Buzz always denied doing anything wrong, and that I should not believe the lies "someone" was spreading. He told me that if I no longer trusted him that he would have to resign. I told him that I did not trust him, and he resigned.

I never told Buzz that Lillian admitted she had made it all up so that Buzz would be fired instead of her.

I should not have believed Lillian. It was the worst mistake of my life.

By confiding in Miles, my father had made another error in judgment. He failed to realize that Miles and I were not just business associates but close personal friends. Ever since Pat and I met Miles and Judy Godin years before, we had a long and close personal relationship.

Although my father had sworn Miles to secrecy on pain of losing the Fuller Tool account, Miles immediately told me the whole sordid story.

To protect Miles, I never told anyone that my father had known for some time that I had been falsely accused of theft and other things.

To this day, my two sisters and their children believe that I stole merchandise from the family business and had resigned in disgrace.

By the time my father confided in Miles, it was irrelevant and too late. I had long since moved on and my relationship with my sisters had already been broken beyond caring.

When I resigned in 1967, my father promptly eliminated me from his will. Years later, after he learned that Lillian had lied, I was put back in his will, although not with a share equal to his two daughters.

With no one to lead the family business into the twenty-first century, Fuller Tool Company, as a family-owned business, did not survive.

Epilogue

Looking back over the years, I take satisfaction in having created good-paying jobs for hundreds of people.

Award Hand Tools Inc. 1965–1967
Omega Precision Tools Inc. 1967–1984
Hand Care Inc. disposable gloves 1984–2009

Life at ninety years plus means enjoying lunch at the club and nine holes of golf with my ninety-seven-year-old buddy, Sandy Epstein; surfing the internet, reading *The New York Times*, e-books, going to the gym, a Netflix movie, tracking my investments, and, of course, a short nap in the afternoon and dinner with friends.

While I am fortunate to have lived a productive and generally healthy life (up to this writing), it is painfully obvious that I cannot "keep up" with people only five years younger.

On the other hand, I have no problem keeping up "mentally" with people half my age. That's a blessing.

I love watching my grandson Max grow up, and am glad to be able to help David, Rachel, Susan, and Julie when, and if, needed.

Here are a few things that did not exist when I was a kid in Brooklyn.
Robots and drones for commercial and personal use
iPhones in use by almost everyone (except Pat F.)
TV sets that stream movies and hundreds of video channels

3D devices worn over the eyes and used to train surgeons
Cars that drive automatically, and stop before hitting anyone
Cars that run on rechargable batteries, or even hydrogen
Solar panels on buildings provide free electricity
Alternate energy sources, including wind, tidal, and nuclear
AI and quantum computing coming soon

Eventually, I assume, we will harness various carbon-free energy sources before our planet is irredeemably destroyed due to climate change.

Unfortunately, in today's world, personal stories of ordinary people are still quite rare. If anyone besides a future family member is interested in my personal story, fifty years from now, it will be surprising.

Evidence of a Stable Lifestyle:

Happily married to Pat Fuller sixty-eight years
Steve Gutman, my friend for seventy-two years
Member of Pine Hollow Club sixty-two years
In the same house in Rolsyn sixty-one years
Gym workouts three times a week for sixty years
The same barber (Jimmy) for sixty-two years
Will soon be ninety-oneyears old (if all goes according to plan)